George Junkin

Political Fallacies

An examination of the false assumptions, and refutation of the sophistical

reasonings, which have brought on this Civil War

George Junkin

Political Fallacies
An examination of the false assumptions, and refutation of the sophistical reasonings, which have brought on this Civil War

ISBN/EAN: 9783337402785

Printed in Europe, USA, Canada, Australia, Japan

Cover: Foto ©Suzi / pixelio.de

More available books at **www.hansebooks.com**

POLITICAL FALLACIES:

AN

EXAMINATION OF THE FALSE ASSUMPTIONS,

AND

REFUTATION OF THE SOPHISTICAL REASONINGS,

WHICH HAVE BROUGHT ON

THIS CIVIL WAR.

BY

GEORGE JUNKIN, D.D., LL.D.

NEW YORK:

CHARLES SCRIBNER, 124 GRAND STREET.

1863.

CONTENTS.

INTRODUCTION.

Tнıs little book, as its title intimates, has for its immediate design the exposure of the leading fallacies which lie at the root of the great conspiracy, and have conduced to its success. By their means the conspiracy realized its design in rebellion, and led on, probably contrary to the expectations of its plotters, to civil war, with all its fearful consequences. It was not the intention of the author to give a history of the conspiracy, the rebellion, or the war; and he has consequently only introduced so much as was necessary to render intelligible the refutation of the sophistical arguments by which the work of blood-shedding has been extended over this vast country.

The ulterior and chief object of the book is to exhibit these groundless assumptions and false reasonings, so as to enable the candid reader to break away from the snares so well adapted to entangle him, to discover where the truth lies, and to recover his standing, if, indeed, he had lost it, or was likely to lose it, and fix himself immovable upon the rock, and thus to

promote a return to the ark of our safety—the CONSTI-
TUTION and the UNION.

As the book is designed not for readers only who
have thoughts, but also, and indeed more especially, for
those who *think*, it does not indulge in poetic flights
and array its sentiments in elegant drapery. It affects
the simplest style, and hopes it uses the language of
common sense.

It is necessary to crave the reader's indulgence at
the outset to a little personality, I might say egotism,
which seems indispensable to enable him to understand
what comes before him. I removed from Lafayette
College, Easton, Penn., in November, 1848, to Washington College, Lexington, Va. This institution was
founded by the Hanover Presbytery in 1774–'5, under
the rectorship of Rev. Wm. Graham, then late of Dau-
phin County, Penn. It was endowed by Washington,
who gave to it certain stocks in the James River
Canal, which were sold, and the proceeds, $50,000,
invested in Virginia State securities. In this institution the author served, according to his feeble ability,
twelve and a half years, with great comfort to himself
and his household. His salary was ample and satisfactory—his surroundings were such, all the time, as always to call forth gratitude to the kind Providence
which had led him to that most beautiful locality and
most inviting field of labor. He doubts not but his services were made, by Divine favor, a blessing to the
church and the community at large. There, as in

every other field of labor, the main purpose of his heart, when in 1830 he surrendered his pastoral charge in the forks of the Susquehanna, and devoted himself to education, viz., to assist in bringing young men into the ministry of the church, was largely realized. Three of his children remain in Rockbridge, and one is not, for the Lord took her away from the evil to come. There he was called upon, for the second time, to purchase his cave of Machpelah, that he might bury his dead out of his sight; there he made the sacred deposit, first, of one who had sojourned by his side for nearly thirty-five years; then of his second daughter, Mrs. Jackson; then of a noble and dearly beloved son-in-law; then of the sweet and lovely boy who soon followed his father; and there he had reserved a plot of ground, three feet by six, for himself. Sixteen miles northeast from Lexington, one son was settled as pastor of a large and most intelligent and comfortable church; ten miles southwest another son, similarly situated, and his oldest daughter located beside him in Lexington.

But otherwise, oh! how far otherwise, had the Lord arranged the matter! Calhoun's sophistry prevailed. The bloody fallacies brought on secession, rebellion, civil war, peradventure—my heart shudders at the conception—peradventure, servile war. From all these delightful surroundings I had my choice to fly, or, abiding, to succumb to the approaching despotism. True, Virginia had twice voted against secession. The Bell and Everett electors were run in by a plurality vote;

1*

add to this the Douglas democratic vote, and the majority was crushing against secession. Then, in the election for members of the convention, the Union vote was a triumphant majority: about two thirds of the convention were union men. In Rockbridge county, the average secession vote was less than one in eleven votes. Yet, notwithstanding all this, I saw plainly that if I remained, absolute silence, or a voice in favor of secession, must be the price of my personal safety. This price was too great for me to pay. It would bankrupt my self-respect and pollute my conscience. The only alternative was flight; and so, leaving my books and furniture to the mercy of Mr. Benjamin's confiscation law, as expounded by himself, I took time by the forelock, and crossed the Potomac at Williamsport after dark on the 9th of May, 1861, having driven the last thirty-five miles, from Winchester, without stopping to feed my horses. To gratify my friends and state the real facts of the case truly, the following narrative was published; and I append it hereto, just as it is, as containing evidence of the most kindly feelings, and affording a good hope that when the storm of war shall have passed, there will be a general return to the same; and also as a fitting general introduction; adding only a note or two to the original publication. With these remarks I submit the little book to the kind guardianship of Heaven and the candid judgment of the American people.

The following was drawn up at its date, and published for the satisfaction of the author's friends; its circulation was, however, limited, and it may prove useful, as leading to a correct understanding of my removal from Virginia.

[For the Standard.]

EXODUS OF DR. JUNKIN.

Mr. Editor:—The following is no Parthian arrow, but a simple history, designed to correct misapprehension and let my friends in Virginia and Pennsylvania know the truth in reference to MY EXODUS from the former to the latter.

In the month of February last I took up the Constitution of the United States for exposition to the Senior Class in Washington College, Va., of which I was then president, using Sheppard's excellent little work as a text-book. This was an anticipation of some two months, in accordance with the desires of the class and my own convictions of duty, in reference to the dangerous misconstructions of that highest production of human genius. I wished, by a fair and honest exposition, to convince my young friends that UNION preceded *Independence*, and even the *Articles of Confederation;* much more the present *Constitution;* that neither the Continental Congress nor the Articles of Confederation created and constituted a *Government:* they had neither supreme, legislative, judicial, nor executive powers. The Congress was simply a grand Committee of the States, exercising many powers of sovereignty, but by no means all that belong to national sovereignty. In these lectures I dealt largely with the archives published by United States authority, reading from them to sustain my positions, and especially from the minutes of the Convention that formed the Constitution, passing through the entire volume, and demonstrating the fact of *union* as the leading principle—the polar star recognized by these wise men of the west, from the very first meeting in this city in September, 1774, and again in May, 1775. I showed that they felt themselves a unit—they recorded themselves a unit: as the United Colonies they appointed and commissioned George Washington as Commander-in-chief, in whose commission the phrase "United Colonies" occurs three several times. My object, in these extended preparatory discussions, was to rivet the conviction in the minds of these dear young men, that UNION was always the master thought in the minds of American patriots; that UNION was the basis of all their actions; that without UNION there could be no *freedom*, no *national government*, no *independence*. From this position, it follows irrefragably, that there never existed a State sovereignty; the supreme power is in the States UNITED: no State ever declared itself an independent nation—none was ever recognized by any power on earth as an independent sovereignty; the doctrine of State rights, or State sovereignty outside of the limits of State constitutions and the lines of demarcation fixed in the United States Constitution, is necessarily subversive of the national government, as General Jackson proved in his proclamation to the people of South Carolina, and from this follows the doctrine which he affirmed, that "disunion by armed force is treason." The right of secession is a national wrong. Hence, I reach the conclusion, by the eternal principles of logic, that "secession" is the essence of all immorality; it neutralizes the highest obligations. Accordingly, the senators of Virginia and others proclaimed the doctrine, that their oath was null and void—they owed no allegiance to the government of the United States.

But in the progress of these discussions I observed a growing restiveness among the students; heard myself called a "Pennsylvania Abolitionist," and saw written on the column opposite my recitation-room door "Lincoln Junkin."

About the close of March, a Palmetto flag was placed on the centre building of the college, surmounting the wooden statue of Washington, on whose head they had nailed a fool's-cap. In this process, led on by a Georgia student, the copper lightning rod was bent, and subsequently broken off. For a student to go out on the roof has always been an offence, punished by demerit. This flag I ordered the servants to take down and bring to me. I was asked what I would do with it, and replied, "burn it after evening prayer." But whilst I was at dinner, they procured a ladder, climbed into the window of my lecture room, and took the flag away.

About a week after it was again erected. I immediately ordered the servants to take it down, and at an hour when all except the Freshmen were at their recitations; these stood about as spectators, and asked what I was going to do with it. I answered, "I'll show you." I ordered the servants to hold the but of the flag pole firmly, and throw the top over from the chapel roof, which is a story lower than the centre building. When the flag came within reach, I stepped up and took some matches out of my pocket, set it on fire, and when it blazed up told the servants to throw the pole out from the building, and whilst it flamed up, I said, "*So perish all efforts to dissolve this glorious Union!*" *

On the 15th of April, my lecture-room door was much injured by attempts to break it open with a strong iron bar. The library door they succeeded in forcing open. The object was to procure the jointed ladder, which the servants had put behind the amphitheatre for safe keeping. (A door opens between the library room and my lecture room.) On the mor-

---

* It is worthy of special notice here, that the young men who were chiefly active in the erecting of these flags perished on July 21, 1861, in the first battle of Bull Run. Two of them were killed by one cannon shot, and a third (and he the leader) perished from excessive over-exertion in carrying his wounded companion three miles to the railroad car. This companion breathed his last just as they were lifting him on the car. And thus, to a melancholy and fearful extent, has the malediction prophetic been accomplished. I am to this day—Dec. 9, 1862—but very imperfectly informed on the subject, by reason of the rebellion cutting off all intercourse between me and my two sons and daughter in Rockbridge; but from all I have heard, I am painfully impressed with the belief that more than fifty per cent. of all those misguided youth who were active in rebelling against me have paid the forfeit of their folly by the sacrifice of their lives. This is cause of unfeigned sorrow; for a very large proportion of them were youth of remarkable promise for talents, diligence in study, purity of moral and religious character; who, but for these bloody fallacies would have lived long and adorned the higher walks of professional life.

ning of the 17th, I saw a disunion flag surmounting the statue
of Washington and the lightning rod.   After prayer I detained
the members of the Faculty, and waved my hand to the students to retire.   I stated to my colleagues that this thing must
be stopped, &c.   One of them said he had just received a petition on the subject, signed by most of the students.   I asked
him to read it.   The substance (I have not a copy) of it was,
that the flag which they had erected might be permitted to
remain.   I stated to the Faculty that it had been placed there
in violation of law, and in contemptuous resistance to my express order, and, of course, if they would grant the prayer of
the petition, my course of duty was clear and plain—I could
not be coerced, but would instantly secede; and left them to
deliberate, and let me know their decision.

At eleven o'clock, the usual hour, the Junior class came
into my room.   I asked whether the flag was on the top of
the College, and received an affirmative answer.   "Then,
gentlemen," said I, "I am under the necessity of assuring you
that I cannot submit to this kind of coercion," and dismissed
them.   One rushed toward the door, shouting, "Thank God
for that! thank God for that!"* and yelled his utmost, in
which he was joined by a few others.

At twelve o'clock, when the Seniors came in, I read to
them the substance of what I had said to the Juniors, and
which, meanwhile, to be sure of the identical words, I had
written down as follows:

"'Is the flag still on the top of the College?'

"Answer, 'Yes.'

"'Well, then, gentlemen, as you put it there in express
opposition to my order, I am under the necessity of telling
you that I have never been ridden over rough shod in that
style, and I never will be; therefore, I never will hear a reci-
tation or deliver a lecture under a rebel flag.   The class is
dismissed.'

"*April* 17, 1861."

* Killed at Bull Run, as I learned shortly after from a Richmond
paper.

They rose and withdrew in the most gentlemanly and respectful manner, with every appearance of sincere regret.

In the evening of the same day, I received from my colleagues a paper, of which the following is a copy, viz:

"W. College, *April* 17, 1861.

"*Action of the Faculty in relation to the Flag on the College Buildings.*

"Whereas the students, in reference to the tidings that the Virginia Convention are about to adopt an ordinance of secession, have hoisted a Southern flag upon the college building, and have made a respectful request of the Faculty that they would permit it to remain; and whereas the Faculty have assurance that this act has not taken place in any *desire to violate* college laws, or offer indignity to any member of the Faculty—an assurance given by the students themselves to a member of the Faculty, and confirmed by the fact that they promptly took down, at the request of the Faculty, a similar flag, erected on a former occasion; and whereas Dr. Junkin regards this act as a wilful violation of law and a personal indignity, and requires the Faculty to have it removed at once, on penalty of his resignation—an alternative which the Faculty think that Dr. Junkin has no right to impose, and which we cannot allow to influence our action in the premises, although we are fully determined to sustain the president, or any individual member of our body, in the maintenance of discipline; and whereas the sole object of the faculty is to allay excitement, and ensure good order and attention to study in college, in this time of civil disturbance, believing, as we do, that these ends will be best promoted by not requiring the *immediate* removal of the flag; therefore,

"*Resolved*, That the flag be permitted to remain, at the discretion of the Faculty.

"Copied from the minutes, and communicated to Dr. Junkin by order of the Faculty.

"J. L. CAMPBELL, *Clerk.*"

There is but one point in which there is positive inaccuracy in the above. It is in regard to the flag said to have been taken down at the request of the Faculty.

The flag there referred to was not "a similar flag," (as I was afterward informed, for I never saw it and knew not of its erection until after it was taken down;) it was a *red flag*, and it was not erected on the centre building, but on the building in which my lecture room was. It was therefore entirely different in its significance. And it was not taken down at the request of the Faculty, for the Faculty as such knew nothing about it; it was taken down at the remonstrance, as I understood, of Professor White, for which interposition I felt thankful.* After what had already transpired, neither I, nor the public, could be at any loss to know what was meant by erecting a *red* flag, not on the centre building over the statue of Washington, as had been the others, but over my Lecture Room.

On the next day I called a meeting of the Trustees at 2½ P. M., the earliest hour practicable, on account of the meeting of the Presbytery of Lexington, and of the Superior Court. In urging the Trustees individually to attend, I assured them it would take but a few minutes, for my resignation would be peremptory and absolute, and leave no room for discussion. I mention this circumstance in order to counteract the gross misrepresentations which I have been told have found their way into some of the Richmond papers, but especially, the *Dispatch*.

* The lovely youth who took down this red flag from over my lecture room, perished at the second battle of Bull Run on the 28th of Aug., 1862, aged about eighteen years. He was an ardent Union man —a devoted student, pure minded as the blood of sprinkling ever cleanses sinners here below. A nobler boy never took seat before me in class, during the thirty-one years of my presidency in Colleges. But this accursed rebellion crushes into its ranks the hoary head and the beardless boy, and drags them on to the slaughter. His brother, a former graduate, lost an arm in the same fight, and two others of my dearly beloved young friends, graduates of two years' standing, the pride of their parents, and ornaments to society, fell likewise on the same bloody field. Oh! ye conspirators against our glorious Union and the peace of the world, look at the slaughter you have brought about, and think of the dread tribunal of Eternal Justice.

The Trustees met accordingly, and the Board was opened with prayer, as usual, and my resignation was presented as follows:

"WASHINGTON COLLEGE, *April* 18, A. D. 1861.

"*To the Board of Trustees of Washington College.*

"GENTLEMEN:—I hereby resign the office to which you called me more than twelve years ago.

"Very respectfully

"Your humble servant,

"GEO. JUNKIN, President."

Dr. McFarland took the chair, made a few kind remarks: others were made—especially by Lawyer Davidson, who was quite complimentary; the vote was passed, I shook hands with all the members, many of whom, as well as myself, were overpowered with tender emotions.

Thus, within twenty hours from the time I was informed that my colleagues had determined to permit the secession flag to wave over the head of Washington, my connection with the College which he had so nobly endowed ceased forever.

With pleasure I append the following, which shows truly that no personal ill feeling has ever existed toward me on the part of my late colleagues, as I doubt not they are perfectly aware that my mind is equally free from every emotion inconsistent with our literary and Christian relations. These difficulties have sprung from the false political maxims of Calhounism, which break down all the barriers of moral truth, and are rushing human society into the vortex of anarchy, and which must end in iron-handed despotism.

"WASHINGTON COLLEGE, *April* 18, 1861.

"*Rev. Geo. Junkin, D.D.*

"DEAR SIR:—Although we, your recent colleagues, as members of the Faculty of Washington College, felt it to be our duty, under peculiar circumstances, to pursue a line of policy which you did not approve, and in consequence of which you have felt constrained to resign your connection with the Institution, we wish to say that we were actuated by no feelings of disrespect to you personally, or disregard of the high position you have filled in the College for so many years. And we desire now to express our high regard for your manly virtues as a Christian minister, and as a gentleman of distinguished talents and learning; and to assure you of our entire confidence in your integrity, of our sincere friendly regards for yourself and family, and our earnest prayer that the twilight of your life may be its brightest and happiest period.

" With much esteem, we are very sincerely
" Your friends,

> J. L. CAMPBELL,
> A. L. NELSON.
> JAMES J. WHITE,
> C. J. HARRIS."

Next day after these transactions I set to work in winding up my business, selling my property, paying my debts, &c., and as the ways of public conveyance were then blocked, I purchased a carriage, drove my own horses three hundred and fifty miles to Oxford, Chester County, and came in on the cars from that place yesterday morning.

> " The Lord shall keep thy soul; he shall
> Preserve thee from all ill :
> Henceforth thy going out and in
> God keep forever will."

> GEO. JUNKIN.

PHILADELPHIA, *May* 18, 1861.

POLITICAL FALLACIES.

CHAPTER I.

MAN, A SOCIAL BEING.

THE nature of anything is the sum of its properties. By these only is it known to us; and, unless our knowledge extends to every property, we cannot affirm it to be complete. Who will say he comprehends all the qualities of any one object of human thought? Who will not rather admit that here, at least, we know but in part? No man pretends to know all the properties of light, of caloric, of electricity, of carbon, of any substance whatever; and therefore no man presumes to suspend investigation and forestall and preclude research into the nature of anything. Still, to us practically, the sum of its *known* properties is the nature of that thing. To these we give names, so that each quality has its proper term, by the use of which we suggest to one another the conception of that particular quality ; and then we invent or appropriate a word to express the general aggregate. It is by this simple process the bounds of knowledge are extended, language is constantly enlarged, and science is improved. Observation and experience furnish the particulars, and the mind classifies and arranges them into a system ; and thus, as the eye of observation runs to and fro, knowledge is increased.

Nor is there any object of the mind's attention more complex and more difficult than man himself. His physical organization holds him in relations to all physical science ; whilst his intellectual and moral qualities open up a vast, a boundless field for investigation. And there is no study more important, more dignified, and attended with more profitable results, when pursued in the spirit of true philosophy, than man himself. On this field, when we turn our eye of observation, the *social* property arrests our attention. Turn whichever way we may, this characteristic looms forth ; and the graphic accuracy of the sacred historian is demonstrated, when he remarks, that " it is not good that the man should be alone ; I will make him a help suitable for him,"—or, as better in the margin, a help *as before him*, in his presence, always with him—

strongly expressing the idea of close, intimate social relations. Beautiful as is the poetic imagery, there is more truth than poetry in the assertion that

> " Eden was a wild,
> And man, the hermit, sighed, till woman smiled."

Thus the divine history of our origin coincides precisely with the universal induction from the facts of all history, that man's nature is social ; and both force upon our convictions the belief that this social quality is an original element implanted by his Creator. Society is a felt necessity of his being, concreated with him. Without it he would not be man at all. This we have evinced in numerous instances. If a human creature have lost it ; if the law of social life is gone ; if the creature turn recluse and misanthrope ; if he ignore society, society ignores him, denies his humanity, treats him as an animal, and shuts him up as a wild and dangerous beast.

Thus, in a two-fold sense, is God the Author of human society. First, in that He created the social element in our nature as a primary law, which necessitates the existence of society ; and secondly, in that He put this law into actual operation in the organization of the social body.

These things being so, it follows, by inevitable

logical necessity, that society does not owe its existence to any supposed voluntary compact. The phrase *social compact* is often used in such connections as to imply this erroneous idea. The theory it suggests seems to be this : that men are created and thrown upon the earth as individuals, in a dissociate condition—bound together by no moral ties, but every man an automaton, subject to the action of his own will ; that in process of time they volunteer to institute society; they form a covenant, agreement, or *compact*, and bind themselves to live together in society : this voluntary agreement is the social compact, and now, after it is constituted, the parties, formerly entirely insulated, are bound together and lie under various obligations which did not before exist. (See Blackstone, I. i.)

Such seems to be the philosophical *theory ;* against it I array the foregoing facts. If God created man social and put him into society, then is this theory entirely without foundation. But, secondly, I object to it, because there is no fact in the history of the race to sustain it. Where and at what period have individuals ever existed in such a condition of insulation ? If this is preposterous figment, I object, in the third place, that no man is ever asked whether he is willing to become a member of society or not. There is no such thing now, and there never was, as *voluntarily* entering into society and coming under the *social compact*. All men are placed in society, as the first pair were, by the immediate act of their Creator. They are born members of society, under protection of its laws, in whose enactment they had no agency ; they live subject to its laws, and can live nowhere else ; they die under the same laws. Private associations, indeed, for specific purposes, are formed voluntarily ; but this is not *civil society*. True, also, men may change their location, may remove from one country to another voluntarily, but this is not creating society by compact.

But, fourthly, no man has a right, at his own option, to leave society and renounce its obligations and discard its duties. I say the *right*, the *moral power*, he has not. The physical power he possesses. He can destroy his life : he can do it by a single blow, or by a number of acts. He can retire from all intercourse with his fellows ; but he cannot *live* in that state ; he must and will pay the forfeit, not of his breaking his voluntary compact with man, but of his rebellion against God in the violation of the social laws which He created in him. He will die.

A compact, therefore, in the ordinary sense of the term—an agreement voluntarily entered into by parties binding themselves by obligations to duties not before existent—such a *social compact* never had any existence, and never can. It is simply a figment of false philosophy; and it ignores the government of God, abnegates the universal law of love, subverts all government over man, and plunges the universe into the chaos of dark, cheerless atheism.

Indeed, we might, perhaps, with profit, take another step on this road of sound philosophy, and affirm that man cannot, by any merely voluntary act of his own, create—give existence to, any moral obligation whatever. The Creator alone can prescribe duties. He that made the moral machine and He only can dictate the laws for its government. Abstractly, this assumes the aspect of a self evident proposition, and yet, in some practical points of view, it will be called in question. We will be asked, Cannot a man bind himself by promise, contract, oath voluntarily taken? What becomes of the business of society? How could it progress if promissory notes were not binding? Before the promise was made there was no obligation of duty, and how is it afterward?

These are plausible objections; but let us see whether they be substantial. And let us be sure where the difficulty lies. Is it not precisely here?

in the interchange of antecedent and consequent ? An adroit, but inadvertent substitution of effect for cause and cause for effect ? Is not the promise to pay a sum, at a given time, based upon a preëxistent obligation ? Will any man promise to pay if he is under no obligation ? Why, on the very face of the note this question is answered—"for value received." This, in the nature of the transaction, precedes the promise. For value received I promise to pay, and if there has been no value received, there is no obligation—the bond is null. Prove against the *pro quo*, and no *quid* follows. Destroy the antecedent and you destroy the consequent. Clearly it is not the promise that creates the obligation, but the preëxistent obligation that creates the promise. The duty—the obligation to do something, springs from the law which God has established for the regulation of human rights. He holds every man responsible for every item of property which His Providence throws into his hands ; " occupy till I come ; " and no man has a right to part with any property, but for a consideration ; and whenever that consideration, in course of Providence, has been given, the duty to pay the equivalent lies ; and therefore the promise follows whenever it is not convenient to discharge the obligation

2

at present. The *duty* is father to the promise, and
not *vice versa*.

The same may be evinced by raising the question, Can a man bind himself—can he make it his
duty, simply by a voluntary promise on oath, to do
a wrong thing ?   Herod decided in the affirmative,
when for his oath's sake he beheaded John in prison.
But was his decision right ?   Was his promise binding ?   More than forty men bound themselves under a curse to kill Paul.   About the same number
took an oath to kill Lincoln at the Camden depot,
Baltimore ; was the promise and the oath binding ?
Did it become their *duty* to do this thing ?   How
is it now with the thousands of knights, who are
under oath to break up the Union ; is it their duty
to perpetrate this enormous wickedness, because
forsooth they have sworn to do it ?

Clearly, then, it is not the voluntary promise or
oath, that creates the duty ; but it is the *duty*, that
renders the promise and the oath right and proper.
The Author of our moral nature is the Author also
of all the laws which are prescribed for its government.   His requisition alone defines duty.   His
will made known to man is supreme.   " My meat
is to do the will of him that sent me."   Man's will
can create no law, prescribe no duty ; but the perfection of his moral character consists in the sub-

ordination of his will to God's. The child is in *duty* bound to obey the parent, not simply *because* the parent commands, but because God commands.

From these views, we learn that *expatriation* is a duty and a right ; or is a sin and a wrong, just as you understand the term. If you take it in the native force of this Latin word—removing from one's country, and transferring one's allegiance from the government under which he was born, to another country and government—this is a privilege, a right, and, under certain providential arrangements, becomes a *duty*. If my condition in the country of my birth, is such that I cannot enjoy life ; cannot secure the happiness of my family ; cannot advance the good of man and the glory of his Maker, as well as I could by removing to another country, then it is my *duty* to expatriate. My *duty* is not created by my will and wishes, but by Divine Providence. My agency in the premises consists simply in the exercises of my reason and judgment. Conscience is to me the interpreter of providence and its well digested decision is the voice of God, binding it upon my soul as a solemn duty to obey.

But if by expatriation be understood, removal from human society—renouncing all government and turning recluse ; then the matter has already been

decided ; no such right exists, for no man can possibly have a right to do wrong.

Much blood and treasure were expended, during
the war of 1812–'15, in consequence of the Bullish
blunder of the British philosophers, in confounding
these two uses of the term *expatriation*. 'Once a
subject—citizen, member of the body politic—always
a subject.' This is true, if by body politic be meant
human society : but false, if the British nation and
government, or any particular nation, be understood : and this was the sense they transferred
to the other and assumed its truth. And this blunder in logic dyed the ocean, lakes and lands in blood,
and eventuated in the glorious winding up on the
8th of January, 1815. Such are some of the legitimate results of the war waged by John Locke,
George Campbell, and others of Britain's most
learned men, upon the syllogism : for after logic
was beaten down by perversions of her doctrines, in
the hands of England's great philosophers, sophistry,
under the leading strings of the cotton thread,
stepped in and controlled the destinies of that
mighty empire. Whether the revival of logic, under
the auspices of Whately and Hamilton, shall succeed in unwrapping the sea island fibre from the
British brain, and breaking the meshes of the arach-
noid web, remains to be seen. Certain it is, *that*

fallacy has spread desolation over a large part of the earth ; and an analogous sophism is now aiming its deadly shafts at the life of the Great Republic, and the vitals of human society. He that repudiates Logic is an enemy to social man.

CHAPTER II.

To forestall a part of those fallacies which spring from the double or vague meaning of words, we may find our account in defining these two terms. It is a curious and singular fact that Blackstone, in his chapter on Rights, gives us no definition, except in his classification and enumeration. He divides rights into *absolute* and *relative*—by the former meaning those that belong to individuals *as men* ; by the latter those which are incident to them as *members of society* ; "such as would belong to their persons merely in a state of nature, and which every man is entitled to enjoy, whether out of society or in it." "The absolute rights of man, considered as a free agent, endowed with discernment to know good and evil, and with power of choosing those measures which appear to him to be most desirable, are usually summed up in one general appellation, and denominated the natural liberty of mankind. This natural liberty consists properly in a power of acting as one thinks fit, without any restraint or control, unless by the law of nature ; being a right inherent in us by birth, and one of the gifts of God to man at his creation, when he endowed him with the faculty of free will. But every man, when he enters into society, gives up a part of his natural liberty, as the price of so valuable a purchase." We have already seen that all this is purely fiction. Such a state of natural rights and liberty never had any existence. But you will observe, he merges *absolute rights* into *natural liberty* and then tells us, " This natural liberty consists properly in a power of acting as one thinks fit, without any restraint or control, unless by the law of nature." But now we put the question, is not this *law of nature* the law of God, concreated with us, and is not this the very law of our social nature, under which man was and is now created ? What then becomes of the " out of society" theory ?

Besides, it is utterly untrue that the savage state is the natural state of man and the truly *free* state, as is implied by this theory. " Natural liberty," being here the savage condition, its assertion is an impeachment of divine wisdom. Did God place man at first in " that wild and savage liberty ? " Was this wild and savage liberty " one of the gifts of God to man at his creation ? " And yet before he can become anything but a wild savage, he must give up this " gift of God," this " wild and savage liberty," in order to enter into society and to make civil liberty possible !

Still we have no definition of *Rights*. What is a right ?   If we view this as a question of physics and inquire, Do five and seven make fifteen ? Are the three angles of a triangle together equal to two right angles ?   Am I on the right road to Lexington ? right is equivalent to *true*, to *correct*. Affirmative answers to the last two questions are *right;* negative to the first is *right*, i. e., *true;* the predicate agrees with the subject of the propositions respectively, or disagrees.

But if we use the word also within the sphere of morals, and say, to love my neighbor is *right;* to disobey the command of God is not *right;* resistance to civil magistrates in the due exercise of their authority is not *right :* in all such cases there is reference to a standard or rule of action."   " Law, in its most general and comprehensive sense, signifies a rule of action "—Blackstone.   This definition is *right—true*, the predicate agrees with the subject. And so in the moral sense, there is always a rule of action referred to when the word *right* is used ; and the agreement or disagreement of the conduct of a moral agent with the rule is the theory affirmed or denied. Honor thy father and mother, this is *right;* it is consonant with the rule of action prescribed by due authority. *Right* is acting according to law. But law is the *will* of God made known to us for the guidance of our conduct. Conformity with law is *right,* and when a moral agent conforms entirely his conduct with the laws prescribed to him, this viewed abstractly is properly called righteousness.

A right action being one conformed to the law, we may rightly say, the actor had a *right* to perform it, i. e., the lawgiver laid it upon him as a *duty.* And thus we come at once, as it were abruptly, to a right definition of duty, i. e., a thing due, which must be done—which the law requires me to do. Thus we reach the doctrine, that rights and duties are reciprocal. Law is the basis and measure of rights. Whatever it commands I have a *right* to do, and nothing more. No man has a right to do what the law forbids ; it would not be right but wrong. *Rights,* therefore, are the things which the Supreme Lawgiver commands us to do ; and *duties* differ from rights only as to the point from which they are viewed. The right proceeds from the Lawgiver, and the duty is the action required to proceed from the subject of law. Nothing can be a right which has not its corresponding

2*

duty. God is the author of all rights ; man is the agent of all duties.

From this, it is but a step to obtain the true idea of liberty ; if the divine command creates and measures all rights, then full and perfect compliance is the using up of all our rights. Obedience to law is the perfection of freedom.

> " He is a free man whom the truth makes free;
> All else are slaves beside."

Would you—the question has been often propounded—" would you submit to a Black Republican ? Would you submit to Lincoln ? " No ! never—nor to any man that ever God made ; but I will submit to the constitution and laws of my country, because they embody the will of God as the rule of action to this nation : and submission to them is perfect liberty.

This doctrine of rights relieves us from some anomalous positions held by moral philosophers. Even so late and so sound an author as Wayland applies the term right so as to cover the most outrageously wrong actions, with but a slight qualification. A man has a right, so far as his neighbor is concerned, to worship an idol. In the chapter on the Sabbath, this principle is advanced ; and it is assumed, that what I have no power to prevent him from doing, my neighbor has a right to do. I cannot prevent him from worshipping an idol and he has a right to do it. The phraseology is unfortunate ; the principle it suggests, of course, he does not justify.

CHAPTER III.

FROM the social nature of man spring the necessity and the fact of government. No state of human society has ever been without it. The most artificial and the farthest removed from the primitive or natural state is not without government. Savages have indeed few laws and few rulers, but some they always have. Theirs is, in the highest sense, the *lex non scripta* of Blackstone. Still, law exists in the rudest, and, as I contend it is, the least free condition. It cannot be conceived, that intelligent beings, endowed with reason and will and a social nature, could act out the principles of their nature without rules of order, by which to regulate their intercourse. Nor can it be conceived that, when they become vastly numerous, they could sustain their intercourse without any special agency for the application of these rules to society. Now this gives us the idea of government—the application of truth to the subject or thing governed, that is, here, the truths of law furnished by his Creator. Government is the agency which social man employs to direct, restrain, control its members by rule and law. " Upon these two foundations, the law of nature and the law of revelation, depend all human laws ; that is to say, no human laws should be suffered to contradict them." *Blackstone*, sec. 2. Men may, and, by reason of the defect of human reason, do often differ as to what the law of nature and of revelation is ; but, all over, it is agreed that the will of God made known for that purpose is the supreme law to man. The twofold method, above referred to, of its communication, varies not its binding force. Whether revealed in man's inner consciousness and his reasonings from data furnished by Providence to outward observation (which constitute *natural religion*, and are equivalent, rather identical, with " the law of nations"), or communicated to us in language, written or spoken, there is no difference in their obligations. The sum of duty of every governing agency is their application to social man for the regulation of his conduct.

It is usual to connect the term " civil " with both society and with government. This is derived from the Romans, and has its origin in the obvious fact that men closely connected in cities were laid under the necessity of organizing governments sooner than when living in a loose and scattered condition. The more frequent the intercourse of society, the more of detail became necessary both in the ramifications of law and in the agencies of its execution. Towns, then, being necessarily ahead of country places in this respect, the epithet *civilis* became attached to their more detailed rules of conduct. We see the same proofs passing before our eyes : as towns fill up and enlarge, subdivisions of law become necessary and therefore common.

We moreover have another use for the epithet *civil;* it is used to contradistinguish those laws which relate solely to secular, earthly, worldly affairs, from such as are of a religious or a spiritual character ; we have laws *civil*, and laws *ecclesiastical* or *spiritual.* We have *civil* society and *religious* society ; *civil* government and *ecclesiastical* or *church* government. And these, both and equally, are of Divine origin, though not of equal extent. The religious element, indeed, is found in the original laws of our social nature, and is, therefore, an essential item in the law of nature and of nations ; but the revealed law laid down in Holy Scripture, besides its clear exhibition of the law of nature, contains, as its main element, the doctrines of grace, of which the primary law gives us no information at all. Now, it is this last, this Gospel revelation (which it is the grand end of the *lex scripta* to make known), that creates the difference in extent of the *civil* and the *ecclesiastical* government. The voluntary reception of the revealed doctrines is necessary to place the recipient under its authority and protection, and to guarantee its rights, whereas all mankind are by nature under the law written in the heart, as Paul designates the law of nature.

This *civil government*, consisting of the laws prescribed by the Creator, and the agency by which they are applied for the regulation of human conduct, is *ordained of God.* I can see no difference in this regard between government *civil* and government *ecclesiastical.* Both and equally are *jure divino.* With the former we have now to do. And little need be added, by way of proof, if the principles already laid down are correct. Even as to the mode of their communication we may not add another word. But as to the appointment of the agency,—the king, the president, the governor, &c.,— this must come up hereafter. The fact of the Divine authority must detain us a moment. And there are two modes of argumentation on the point : from the revealed law and from the facts of providence. The latter maintains, that power actually exercised, by an individual or an association of men, over a

larger number, is evidence of the Creator's will that
so it ought to be. The divine right of kings has
long been affirmed. And this is true, in a strict
and qualified sense. The governing power belongs
to God, and by whomsoever exercised, must be respected and obeyed as Divine law ; but whether the
party by whom it is exercised has a Divine commission, whether the *de facto* governor is also *de jure*,
is another question. Be this as it may, just and
right laws are to be obeyed because they are God's.

And this is the teaching of sacred Scripture :
" Let every soul be subject unto the higher powers,
for there is no power (*exousia*) but of God ; the
powers that be are ordained of God." Rom. xiii.
The Greek word here properly signifies *moral power*
—*rightful authority*. So Solomon, Prov. viii. 15,
16 : " By me kings reign, and princes decree justice
[not injustice]. By me princes rule, and nobles, even
all the judges of the earth." So Dan. iv. 32 : " The
Most High ruleth in the kingdom of men, and giveth it to whomsoever He will." All righteous rule
is from God. So Paul, having affirmed that the
existing powers—authorities for applying the Divine
laws to the regulation of human conduct—are ordained of God, proceeds to the consequences : " Who-
soever, therefore, resisteth the power, resisteth the
ordinance of God, and they that resist shall receive

to themselves damnation. For rulers [archons—supreme magistrates] are not a terror to good works, but to the evil. Wilt thou then not be afraid of the power ? do that which is good, and thou shalt have praise of the same, for he is the minister of God to thee for good. But if thou do that which is evil, be afraid ; for he beareth not the sword in vain ; for he is the minister of God, a revenger [avenger] to execute wrath upon him that doeth evil." Nothing could be more conclusive. The power, the authority to apply the Divine law for the government of men, belongs to the Divine Being. The supreme magistrate (which at this juncture was bloody Nero, for he was now the archon of the Roman world) had no authority to burn Christians or to murder his own friends. Physical force he had (*dunamis*), and that from God ; but only in the same sense that any assassin or Satan himself has—no rightful authority.

Nor is Peter's testimony less explicit, 1, ii. 13, 14 : " Submit yourselves to every ordinance of man for the Lord's sake ; whether it be to the king as supreme, or unto governors, as unto them that are sent by him for the punishment of evil doers and the praise of them that do well." Here is submission very peremptorily enjoined, but not absolute—*for the Lord's sake;* Divine authority in the magistrate is that to which submission is enjoined. If the king, as supreme, as the head archon, order an act of idolatry, he must not be obeyed, for he has no authority for such an order. As the minister, the *deacon*, the executive officer of God, his Master's warrant is wanting ; the order is tyranny, and must not be complied with. Resistance to tyrants is obedience to God. Peter also settles the order of submission : where there are magistrates of different grades, the highest officer must of course be first obeyed ; and this brings us into the margin of another and a distinct field of investigation.

CHAPTER IV.

MERE philological research guides to the true idea here. Webster traces the word back to the Latin, super — supernus, superus, sopranus — through the French, souverain.

" Sovereign. 1. Supreme in power ; possessing supreme dominion ; as a sovereign prince. God is the Sovereign Ruler of the universe.

" 2. Supreme ; superior to all others ; chief."

" Sovereignty — supreme power ; supremacy ; the possession of the highest power, or of uncontrollable power. Absolute sovereignty belongs to God only."

Bouvier's Law Dictionary has it thus : " Sovereignty—The union and exercise of all human power possessed in a state ; it is a combination of all power ; it is the power to do everything in a state without accountability — to make laws, to execute and apply them ; to impose and collect taxes, and levy contributions ; to make war and peace ; to form treaties of alliance or of commerce with foreign nations, and the like."

Vattel : " Nations or states are bodies politic, societies of men united together for the purpose of promoting their mutual safety and advantage by the joint efforts of their combined strength." P. liv.

" Every nation that governs itself, under what form soever, without dependence on any foreign power, is a sovereign state. P. 2.

" It is necessary that there should be established a Public Authority to order and direct what is to be done by each in relation to the end of the Association. This political authority is the *Sovereignty*, and he or they who are invested with it are the sovereign." P. 1.

" By the sovereign power (says Blackstone, Introd., sec. 2), as was before observed, is meant the making of laws ; for wherever that power resides, all others must conform to, and be directed by it, whatever appearance the outward form and administration may put on. * * * In a democracy, where the right of making laws resides in the people at large, public virtue, or goodness of intention, is more likely to be found, than either of the other qualities of government. Popular assemblies are frequently foolish in their contrivance,

and weak in their execution ; but generally mean
to do the thing that is right and just, and have
always a degree of patriotism or public spirit.   In
aristocracies there is more wisdom to be found than
in the other frames of government ; being composed, or intended to be composed, of the most
experienced citizens.   A monarchy is, indeed, the
most powerful of any, all the sinews of government
being knit together, and united in the hand of the
prince ; but then there is imminent danger of his
employing that strength to improvident or oppressive purposes." He then cites the opinion of Cicero,
that a wise and prudent combination of these three
would constitute the best republic—an opinion controverted by Tacitus.   He proceeds to argue the
preëminent superiority of the British Constitution,
because it embodies and exemplifies Cicero's opinion.
" The legislature of the kingdom is intrusted to
three distinct powers, entirely independent of each
other : first, the king ; secondly, the lords spiritual
and temporal, which is an aristocratical assembly
of persons selected for their piety, their birth, their
wisdom, their valor, or their property ; and, thirdly,
the house of commons, freely chosen by the people from among themselves, which makes it a kind
of democracy.

" Here, then, is lodged the sovereignty of the

British Constitution ; and lodged as beneficially as is possible for society. For in no other shape could we be so certain of finding the three great qualities of government so well and so happily united. If the supreme power were lodged in any one of the three branches separately, we must be exposed to the inconveniences of either absolute monarchy, aristocracy, or democracy ; and so want two of the three principal ingredients of good polity, either virtue, wisdom, or power."

It will be noticed here, that the great oracle of English law impliedly, but most emphatically denies that the king *per se* is sovereign of the British nation. The monarch holds only a part of the sovereignty, which is not only divisible, but necessarily divided, wherever freedom dwells. The idea of sovereignty being a unit, and a unit *sui generis*, incapable of division, an atom, a monad—this idea is repudiated : it belongs to a newer philosophy. Its paternity is not much to its praise. Sovereignty is *governing authority* in a state ; as Paul calls it, *exousia;* and there is no *power* but of God. Ruling authority, in human hands, must be distributed ; and the wise tempering of the distribution, the *"sit modice confusa"* of Cicero, will very accurately measure the freedom of a state.

In mechanics, the adjustment of balances is indispensable to the success of the machine. If this is lost, the preponderating force must drive on, to the utter demolition of the whole, from the most delicate structures of the horologist to the engine of ten thousand horse power. Let the balance of centrifugal and centripetal forces be lost, and the solar system becomes a wreck, and Phaeton's fiery car runs riot through a desolated universe. So, in the moral machinery of human government, powers must be so adjusted as to constitute mutual checks upon each other, that all the parts may combine to the perfection of the whole.

For answering the question of location—*where is this power deposited?*—we are already possessed of the material. Daniel (iv. 32), standing in the simple grandeur of Faith and the confidence it generates, before the mightiest monarch on earth, tells him, "The Most High ruleth in the kingdom of men, and giveth it to whomsoever he will." Sovereignty absolute is found only in God : from him alone is it distributed among men. But to whom, and how ? It is scarcely necessary for us to dwell for a moment even upon the *divine right of kings,* as that phrase has been sometimes understood—a *direct* and *immediate* gift from God. It is nowhere maintained that such a grant exists ; not even by those who now hold to the hereditary descent of ruling power. For even these are obliged to run back to a point when the first of any line is reached, at which they admit the authority was not found in the family blood, but was derived to it from the consent of the people. This is clearly admitted in English history, and even more decidedly acknowledged in nations where the Salic law prevails, by which the royal blood even, is excluded whenever it flows only in females' veins.

The people are intrusted with their own government, and their assent or consent is indispensable even to kings and nobles. This idea looms out and irradiates the whole line of history in every nation. "The executive power of the English nation is vested in a single person, by the general *consent* of the people." Blackstone, b. i., c. 3. The only practical difficulty in our way, is the question, How? How does the sovereignty, the power of governing themselves, pass from them to the rulers? *How* does He, who ruleth in the kingdom of men, give His ruling authority to the king, the president, the governor, the sheriff, the police officer? If sovereignty is a franchise from the God who made him, how can man be deprived of it, but by authority of the Giver? Can he rightfully abandon it? Can he bury this precious talent in the earth, and yet escape his responsibility? So far, therefore, from kings and rulers having any immediate right of sovereignty, mankind—those on whom the franchise is bestowed—are under bonds the most solemn conceivable, to maintain and retain it, and yield it only to their own proper agents, to be exercised for their benefit ; and whenever it is abused, so as to destroy its designed end, they are bound to reject these agents, recall the power, and resume its exercise. That is, there exists an ultimate right of rebellion and revolution in the people of every nation, to be resorted to whenever the authority to rule is so abused as to miss entirely its grand end—the welfare of the people.

The methods of this temporary transfer of supreme power, or rather of that part of it which it is right for a people to delegate for a time, are various. If a hundred men and women were thrown upon a desert island, and so cut off from all civil government, it would be both a privilege and a duty to act toward each other according to the social laws to which we have referred. One of their number, suitably qualified, might assume headship, of his own motion. If this assumption be acquiesced in by the rest, he becomes an executive head—perhaps also, in a degree, a legislative head—to the body politic. If one were called by the formal vote of the body, i. e., a majority of the people, to exer-

3

cise a part of the sovereignty, he would be, to all intents, and in all right, a minister of God to that people. His acts, within the sphere of the laws prescribed by the Creator, are those of a civil ruler, or rather a servant of that people ; and he is bound to do and to act for their good : he is *jure divino* an officer, as truly as is the monarch of a hereditary line, swaying a sceptre over a hundred millions of men. In short, it is of little consequence in what form the people's consent to the exercise of any part of sovereignty over them, by any individual, may be expressed. The fact of its expression places that authority in his hands, just to the extent of the concession ; and he is therefore and thereby a magistrate — a minister of God—to that people, during the period designated. In such a transfer and its acceptance, there is compact, covenant, or agreement between the people and the elected ruler or public servant; and usually the question of wages for his service, or salary for office duties, forms an essential part.

CHAPTER V.

THE AMERICAN COLONIES.

THE most striking circumstance in their history is the original moving cause of their inception. Why did so many people tear themselves away from the comforts of Christian and civilized society; and that too in a country where as much of liberty was enjoyed as in any on the globe? Was it that the place of their fathers' sepulchres had become too strait for them?—the population had become too dense for them to gather a comfortable subsistence from the soil? The population of the British Isles was scarcely a tithe of what it is now. Was it that the enticements to these shores, the refinements and felicities of society here, was so much superior to those of their native land? Nothing of the kind. A trackless wilderness lay before them, inhabited only by savage beasts and not less savage men. Why then should they abandon the sweets of home for a strange and barbarous country? Every school-boy has the answer ready: they were borne down by the spirit of religious intolerance. The error of the world, the church, the age, was the idol of uniformity in religious belief. This looms out from all the pages of our colonial history, that religious persecution, disfranchisement, and oppression forced the colonists from the bosom of a misguided church and an unrelenting state into the wilderness. With perhaps the single exception of Virginia, all the colonies were planted by refugees from intolerance. To enjoy liberty of conscience in a wilderness home, seemed to them preferable to a residence in glorious old Albion, under compulsion of bowing the knee to the image of Baal. Virginia was a speculation, originating in commercial cupidity ; Plymouth was a church, persecuted and peeled ; trodden down, and yet not destroyed ; but seeking a refuge from the storm and a covert from the tempest—the shadow of a great rock in a weary land. Not the fostering care, but the cruelty of the mother country planted these colonies ; and her avarice was early displayed in systematic endeavors to reap a revenue from their industry. In Virginia this was exemplified in the efforts of the Stuarts to secure to themselves a monopoly of the tobacco trade. So eagerly did England grasp at the profits of trade, that Charles I. conceded large privileges as a set off for this monopoly. " The plantation," says Bancroft (ii. 194), "no longer governed by a chartered company, was become a royal province, and an object of favor ; and, as it enforced conformity to the Church of England, it could not be an object of suspicion to the church or the court. Franchises were neither conceded nor restricted ; for it did not recur to his pride that at that time there could be in an American province anything like established privileges or vigorous political life ; nor was he aware that the seeds of liberty were already germinating on the borders of the Chesapeake. His first Virginia measure was a proclamation on tobacco, confirming to Virginia and the Somer Islands the exclusive supply of the British market, under penalty of the censure of the star chamber for disobedience. In a few days, a new proclamation appeared, in which it was his evident design to secure the profits that might before have been engrossed by the corporation. After a careful declaration of the features of the charters, and consequently of the immediate dependence of Virginia upon himself, a declaration aimed against the claims of the London company, and not against the franchises of the colonists, the monarch proceeded to announce his fixed resolution of becoming, through his agents, the sole factor of the planters. Indifferent to their constitution, it was his principal aim to monopolize the profits of their industry; and the political rights of Virginia were established as usages by his salutary neglect." Thus, as often happens, one sinful lust devours another; the eagerness of the kings to secure a revenue, conceded a strong protective tariff to the great staple of Virginia; and at the same time unwittingly acknowledged a representative government, and even the occasional election of their own governor to the colonists. Avarice fed the goose that he might eat the eggs and feather his own nest; but the goose became an eagle, and the eggs sent forth a numerous brood, which plucked the crown from its selfish benefactor. "This is the first recognition, on the part of a Stuart, of a representative assembly in America." But the price asked was too great. The planters refused to put themselves in the power of the crown as an absolute monopolist of tobacco, even though the king offered the monopoly of the English market; for obviously, if the king could be the only purchaser, they were at his mercy. Similar efforts were made after the restoration. Cromwell's navigation act, which laid the foundation of England's supremacy on the sea, and of her manufacturing preëminence on land, was variously modified to the disadvantage of colonial commerce. "No vessel, laden with colonial commodities, might sail from the harbors of Vir-

ginia for any ports but those of England, that the
staple of those commodities might be made in the
mother country ; and all trade with foreign vessels,
except in cases of necessity, was forbidden." (Bancroft, i. 221.) This constitutes one of the reasons
in the Declaration—" giving his assent to their acts
of pretended legislation—for cutting off our trade
with all parts of the world." There is perhaps no
one feature of British legislation, in reference to the
colonies, more prominent than this, of securing a
revenue in one or both methods, of direct taxation
and of commercial advantages. All the charters
and grants of every description carefully secure
these interests, and bind the colonies under obligations to the crown and parliament. All her subsequent legislation is shaped with the view to insure
perpetual dependence, both in regard to the manufacture of goods and their exchange. Whether they
understood it may be doubtful, but their policy was
an embodiment of the doctrine so ably set forth in
Mr. H. C. Carey's masterly work, " Social Philosophy," viz., that a people whose industrial energies are
expended wholly in the production of raw materials
to be exported to another country for manufacture
and return, is a colonial dependent of the country
that manufactures and returns them. Manufacturing industry is the civilizer ; raw producers glide

toward semi-barbarism. England's policy ever has been to hold her colonies in this position : if she has not succeeded, it has not been for want of effort, but because of the natural tendency of man, and especially of the Anglo-Saxon race, toward the development of the human powers. To check this in America and to stimulate it in Britain has been her master policy for three hundred years.

Division of labor, so necessary an element in a people's large development by mechanical industry and progress, has its basis in diversities of soil and climate, and this springs from the inclination of the earth's axis to the plane of its orbit. Thus the Creator makes division of labor a necessity on a large scale ; and commerce is a dependant on diversified pursuits. England's madness consists in her gigantic efforts to become the *ergastulum generale* —the universal workshop of the globe. But as her desperate effort to execute this wild scheme upon her own colonies failed, so will all her efforts to make the nations all colonial dependants.

A capital point in this scheme, as to America, was to hem up the colonies severally within themselves, prevent them from traffic one with the other, and thus cut off all interdependence, by prohibiting, as far as possible, all intercommunication ; and at the same time, and by this very means, to insure the dependence of each upon herself. " Let us," she says, "have your raw materials ; we can manufacture them much cheaper and better than you can ; we will send for them and work them up for you in the most beautiful manner, and return to you as much as each may need." In furtherance of this scheme, she threw every hindrance possible in the way of the colonies becoming skilled in producing for themselves the decencies and luxuries of life. Heavy fines were imposed upon artisans for attempting to emigrate to the colonies, and especially for attempting to remove any implements and machinery. Books were written for America ; and Adam Smith's doctrines were glossed, and are to this day, to mean the opposite of what they do mean, and thus to give the weight of his name against American manufacturing industry and in favor of foreign. Thus, the infants are always to remain helpless and be kept in leading strings, and so dependent on the nurse and the step-mother. They must be kept ignorant of their relations to each other only through their common parent ; and their adaptation to aid each other and bear each other's burdens, by reason of diversities of soil, climates, and productions, must not be improved, lest unions might be formed by their home exchanges detrimental to the dependence of each upon the home government.

3*

CHAPTER VI.

UNION OF THE COLONIES.

THE social laws of his nature, and these only, elevate man and give him dominion over the more powerful animals. Without combination he is weak, and must soon perish from the earth ; but in union there is strength. " Concentrated action is powerful action." The colonies early felt the necessity of consolidation of the members of each into a body politic, and the exercise of that partial or limited sovereignty which they held ; but moreover, of a federative union, to give them strength to resist outward pressure common to them all. The union of their forces in their conflicts with the Indians had taught them its importance ; and "the vicinity of the Dutch, a powerful neighbor, whose claims Connecticut could not, single-handed, defeat, led the colonists of the West to renew the negotiation for a union, and with such success that, within a few years, THE UNITED COLONIES OF NEW ENGLAND were made all as one." (Bancroft,

i. 420.) "The Union embraced the separate governments of Massachusetts, Plymouth, Connecticut, and New Haven; but to each its respective local jurisdiction was carefully reserved. The question of State rights is nearly two hundred years old. [This was in 1643.] The affairs of the confederacy were intrusted to commissioners, consisting of two from each colony."

Passing over several exemplifications of the same character, let us attend for a moment to the case of 1754. A hundred and eleven years of very varied experience had enforced upon the minds of the colonists the importance of the maxim which soon came to be a song in the mouth of every schoolboy: "United we stand, divided we fall." Yea, this conviction had worked itself deeply into the minds of the British nation, for in its conflicts with its "natural enemy," the royal government was made to feel, more than once, that the colonies were an element of strength; for the French were resisted successfully, and could only be successfully resisted and driven from America, by the aid of colonial power coöperating with that of the mother country. Consequently, whilst the cloud of a new French war was lowering in the dim distance, the British Government, departing from their habitual policy of preventing the colonies from intimate connections among themselves, invited a congress of deputies from all the colonies to meet in Albany, New York. "With a view to this end, an order was sent over by the Lords of Trade [trade always governs England], directing that commissioners should be appointed in several of the provinces to assemble at Albany. The immediate object was to conciliate the Six Nations, by giving them presents, and renewing a treaty by which they should be prevented from going over to the French, or being drawn away by the Indians under their influence."

"The day appointed for the assembling of the commissioners was the 14th of June, 1754, at Albany, but they did not meet till the 19th, when it was found that the following colonies were represented, namely, New Hampshire, Massachusetts, Rhode Island, Connecticut, New York, Pennsylvania, and Maryland. The whole number appointed was twenty-five, who all attended. Franklin was one of the delegates from Pennsylvania." (Franklin's Works, vol. iii., p. 22.)

On his way to Albany, Franklin, whose inventive genius was ever on the alert, conceived the idea of a more extended and permanent union of the colonies. If—he seems to have reasoned—if, for repelling the Indians and French, a temporary union by representatives of the northern colonies is

deemed by England to be important, why not en-
hance the importance by a permanent union of all
the colonies ? Can the beneficial effects of combination be only a temporary expedient ? Consequently he drew up a very brief sketch of a plan of
union with a view to permanency. This paper he
left with a friend in New York, with the following
note :

"NEW YORK, *June 8th*, 1754.

" Mr. Alexander is requested to peruse these
Hints, and make remarks in correcting or improving the scheme, and send the paper with such
remarks to Dr. Colden for his sentiments, who is
desired to forward the whole to Albany, to their
very humble servant,   B. FRANKLIN."

" While the Indian business was in progress,"
says Sparks, the historian and editor of Franklin's
works, iii. 23, " the subject was brought before the
convention. Under date of June 24th, the following record is found in the journal :

" A motion was made that the commissioners
deliver their opinion whether a union of all the colonies is not at present absolutely necessary for their
security and defence. The question was accordingly
put and passed in the affirmative *unanimously*."

A committee of one from " each government "

was appointed to digest and report a plan of union. Franklin's sketch is in the words following, namely, "A GOVERNOR-GENERAL, to be appointed by the king; to be a military man; to have a salary from the crown; to have a negation on all acts of the Grand Council, and carry into execution whatever is agreed upon by him and the Grand Council. GRAND COUNCIL:—One member to be chosen by the Assembly of each of the smaller colonies, and two or more by each of the larger, in proportion to the sums they pay into the general treasury. MEMBERS' PAY:— — shillings sterling per diem during their sitting, and mileage for travelling expenses. PLACE AND TIME OF MEETING:— To meet — times in the year, at the capital of each colony, in course, unless particular circumstances and emergencies require more frequent meetings, and alterations in the course of places. The Governor-General to judge of those circumstances, &c., and to call by his writs. GENERAL TREASURY:— Its fund, an excise on strong liquors, pretty equally drank in the colonies, or duty on liquor imported, or — shillings on each license of a public house, or excise on superfluities, as tea, &c. &c. All which would pay in some proportion to the present wealth of each colony, and increase as that wealth increases, and prevent disputes about inequalities of quotas.

To be collected in each colony and lodged in their treasury, to be ready for the payment of orders issuing from the Governor-General and the Grand Council jointly. DUTY AND POWER OF THE GOVERNOR-GENERAL AND GRAND COUNCIL :—To order all Indian treaties. Make all Indian purchases not within proprietary grants. Make and support new settlements, by building forts, raising and paying soldiers to garrison the forts, defend the frontiers, and annoy the enemy. Equip guard vessels to scour the coasts from privateers in time of war, and protect the trade, and everything that shall be found necessary for the defence and support of the colonies in general, and increasing and extending their settlements, &c. For the expense they may draw on the fund in the treasury of any colony. MANNER OF FORMING THIS UNION :—The scheme, being first well considered, corrected, and improved by the commissioners at Albany, to be sent home, and an act of parliament for establishing it."

It will be seen that these *Hints* are the substance of the plan reported by the committee. We shall here present it as adopted by the convention, omitting the exposition and defence of the articles, as presented by Sparks, vol. iii., 32 to 55, with, however, the strong recommendation to the reader that he carefully inspect the whole. I shall number the articles for convenient reference. They first show the weakness and inefficiency of the colonies for want of a common bond, and then come to the unanimous resolution "that a union of all the colonies is absolutely necessary for their preservation." Then, to insure its perpetuity and to forefend secession, they remark: "Yet, as any colony, on the least dissatisfaction, might repeal its act [of entering the union], and thereby withdraw itself from the union, it would not be a stable one, or such as could be depended on; for, if only one colony should, on any disgust, withdraw itself, others might think it unjust and unequal, that they, by continuing in the union, should be at the expense of defending a colony which refused to bear its proportionable part, and would therefore, one after another, withdraw, till the whole would crumble into its original parts." Therefore the commissioners came to another previous resolution, "that it was necessary the union should be established by an act of parliament."

I. PRESIDENT-GENERAL.

That the said general government be administered by a President-General, to be appointed and supported by the crown; and a Grand Council, to be chosen by the representatives of the people of the several colonies met in their respective assemblies.

II. PLACE OF FIRST MEETING.

— who shall meet for the first time at the city of Philadelphia, in Pennsylvania, being called by the President-General as soon as conveniently may be after his appointment.

III. NEW ELECTIONS.

That there shall be a new election of the members of the Grand Council every three years ; and, on the death or resignation of any member, his place should be supplied by a new choice at the next sitting of the Assembly of the colony he represented.

IV. PROPORTION OF MEMBERS AFTER THE FIRST THREE YEARS.

That after the first three years, when the proportion of money arising out of each colony to the general treasury can be known, the number of members to be chosen for each colony shall, from time to time, in all ensuing elections, be regulated by that proportion, yet so as that the number to be chosen by any one province be not more than seven nor less than two.

V. MEETING OF THE GRAND COUNCIL, AND CALL.

That the Grand Council shall meet once in every year, and oftener if occasion require, at such time and place as they shall adjourn to at the last preceding meeting, or as they shall be called to meet at by the President-General on any emergency; he having first obtained in writing the consent of seven of the members to such call, and sent due and timely notice to the whole.

VI. CONTINUANCE.

That the Grand Council have power to choose their speaker; and shall neither be dissolved, prorogued, nor continued sitting longer than six weeks at one time, without their own consent or the special command of the crown.

VII. MEMBERS' ALLOWANCE.

That the members of the Grand Council shall be allowed for their service ten shillings sterling per diem, during their session and journey to and from the place of meeting, twenty miles to be reckoned a day's journey.

VIII. ASSENT OF PRESIDENT-GENERAL, AND HIS DUTY.

That the assent of the President-General be requisite to all acts of the Grand Council, and that it be his office and duty to cause them to be carried into execution.

IX. POWER OF PRESIDENT-GENERAL AND GRAND COUN-CIL; TREATIES OF PEACE AND WAR.

That the President-General, with the advice of the Grand Council, hold or direct all Indian treaties, in which the general interest of the colonies may be concerned ; and make peace or declare war with Indian nations.

X. INDIAN TRADE.

That they make such laws as they judge necessary for regulating all Indian trade.

XI. INDIAN PURCHASES.

That they make all purchases from Indians for the crown, of lands not within the bounds of particular colonies, or that shall not be within their bounds when some of them are reduced to more convenient dimensions.

XII. NEW SETTLEMENTS.

That they make new settlements on such purchases, by granting lands in the king's name, reserving a quitrent to the crown for the use of the general treasury.

XIII. LAWS TO GOVERN THEM.

That they make laws for regulating and governing new settlements, till the crown shall think fit
to form them into particular governments.

XIV. RAISE SOLDIERS AND EQUIP VESSELS, ETC.

That they raise and pay soldiers and build forts
for the defence of any of the colonies, and equip
vessels of force to guard the coasts and protect the
trade on the ocean, lakes, or great rivers; but they
shall not impress men in any colony, without the
consent of the legislature.

XV. POWER TO MAKE LAWS, LAY DUTIES, ETC.

That for these purposes they have power to
make laws, and lay and levy such general duties,
imposts, or taxes, as to them shall appear most
equal and just (considering the ability and other

circumstances of the inhabitants in the several colonies), and such as may be collected with the least inconvenience to the people; rather discouraging luxury, than loading industry with unnecessary burdens.

XVI. GENERAL TREASURE AND PARTICULAR TREASURE.

That they appoint a General Treasurer, and particular treasurer in each government, when necessary; and from time to time may order the sums in the treasury of each government into the general treasury, or draw on them for special payments, as they find most convenient.

XVII. MONEY, HOW TO ISSUE.

Yet no money is to issue but by joint orders of the President-General and Grand Council; except where sums have been appropriated to particular purposes, and the President-General is previously empowered by an act to draw such sums.

XVIII. ACCOUNTS.

That the general accounts shall be yearly settled, and reported to the several assemblies.

XIX. QUORUM.

That a quorum of the Grand Council, empowered to act with the President-General, do consist of twenty-five members ; among whom there shall be one or more from a majority of the colonies.

XX. LAWS TO BE TRANSMITTED.

That the laws made by them for the purposes aforesaid shall not be repugnant, but, as near as may be, agreeable to the laws of England, and shall be transmitted to the king in council for approbation ; and if not disapproved within three years after presentation, to remain in force.

XXI. DEATH OF THE PRESIDENT-GENERAL.

That, in case of the death of the President-General, the speaker of the Grand Council for the time being shall succeed, and be vested with the same powers and authorities, to continue till the king's pleasure be known.

XXII. OFFICERS, HOW APPOINTED.

That all military commission officers, whether for land or sea service, to act under this general constitution, shall be nominated by the President-General ; but the approbation of the Grand Council is to be obtained before they receive their commissions ; and all civil officers are to be nominated by the Grand Council, and to receive the President-General's approbation before they officiate.

XXIII. VACANCIES, HOW SUPPLIED.

But, in case of vacancy by death or removal of any officer, civil or military, under this constitution, the Governor of the province in which such vacancy happens may appoint, till the pleasure of the President-General and Grand Council can be known.

XXIV. EACH COLONY MAY DEFEND ITSELF ON EMERGENCY, ETC.

That the particular military as well as civil establishments in each colony remain in their present state, the general constitution notwithstanding ; and that on sudden emergencies any colony may defend itself, and lay the accounts of expense thence arising before the President-General and Grand Council, who may allow and order payment of the same, as far as they judge such accounts just and reasonable.

On these *Hints* and this *Plan* the reader will make his own comments, whilst I remark :

1. The purpose for which they are adduced they do surely accomplish : they *prove* the deep feeling

conviction of this body, of the indispensable necessity for a UNION of the colonies.

2. They view and speak of the colonies as governments—xiii, xvi—and denominate what they propose the " General Government." (i.)

3. They call this a constitution, a " general constitution." (xxii, xxiii, xxiv.)

4. It creates and involves all the proper powers of a government, except that it establishes no judiciary. Legislative authority is fully recognised, with power to execute their own laws, subject only to the veto of the crown for three years. (xv, xvii, xvii.) In this it goes far beyond " The Articles of Confederation and Perpetual Union," as we shall more fully see hereafter.

5. This Plan of Union bears all the marks of that original genius which produced the *Hints*. Manifestly Franklin was the father of it ; and as he was the only man who sat in the convention, and also, thirty-three years afterwards, in this convention to form our present Constitution, it is impossible to doubt his great weight and influence in infusing the substance of this Plan into the more matured system that now (September 9th, 1862) is to be subverted.

6. England's necessity constrained her to teach to the colonies this great and important lesson of

union in order to strength. The lords of trade, to save money, of course, and to prevent interruption of trade, suggested the *hint* of a union of the colonies in their own defence against France and the Indians, which nineteen years later was matured into a union of the colonies against England and the same Indians.

Let us advert to a few other moves made in this direction. And here it is deeply interesting to notice, by the dates, how almost miraculously the spirit of freedom and union moved the masses at the same moment over all the land. Charleston, S. C., June, 1774, a public meeting having been called and having deliberated, did unanimously agree to "such steps as are necessary to be pursued, in union with the inhabitants of all our sister colonies on this continent, in order to arrest the dangers impending over American liberties in general." (See Amer. Archives, 4th series, vol. i, p. 409.)

Newport, Rhode Island, June 13, 1774, the General Assembly met, and on the 15th passed the following : "Resolve 1st. That it is the opinion of this Assembly that a firm and inviolable union of all the colonies, in counsel and measures, is absolutely necessary for the preservation of their rights and liberties." (P. 416.) The Resolve 2d appoints Samuel Hopkins and Henry Ward "to represent

4

the people of this colony in a general congress of representatives from other colonies," &c.

June 14, 1774, Charles County Court House, Port Tobacco, Md. " Resolve 5th. It is the opinion of this meeting that a congress of deputies from the several colonies will be the most probable means of uniting America in one general measure to effectuate a repeal of the said act of Parliament " (the Boston Port bill).

" At a meeting of the inhabitants of the borough of Lancaster, Penn., at the Court House in said borough, on Wednesday, the 15th day of June, 1774, Agreed, that to preserve the constitutional rights of the inhabitants of America, it is incumbent on every colony to devise and use the most effectual means to procure a repeal of the late act of Parliament against the town of Boston." (P. 415.)

Massachusetts House of Representatives, June 17th, 1774, " do resolve, that a meeting of committees from the several colonies on this continent is highly expedient and necessary. That the Honorable James Bowdoin, Esq., the Honorable Thomas Cushing, Esq., Mr. Samuel Adams, John Adams, and Robert Treat Paine, Esqs., be, and they are hereby appointed a committee on the part of this province for the purposes aforesaid, any three of whom shall be a quorum, to meet such committees or delegates from the other colonies as have been or may be appointed."

Easton public meeting, June 21, 1774. Resolve " 3d. That it is our opinion the most constitutional and effectual method of obtaining such redress, is by having a general congress of committees, to be composed and chosen out of the members of the different assemblies of each colony." (P. 436.)

"Pennsylvania convention, July 15, 1774, Philadelphia. Resolved *unanimously*, That there is an absolute necessity that a congress of deputies from the several colonies be immediately assembled, to consult together and form a general plan of conduct to be observed by all the colonies." (P. 556.)

This resolution was shortly afterward adopted and passed by the Legislature. (P. 606.)

This is a sample and selection of the incipient measures toward a Continental Congress and a union of the colonies. Accordingly the meeting took place. On the 5th of September, 1774, the committees from twelve colonies assembled in the Carpenters' Hall, Chestnut street, Philadelphia. Virginia was represented by Peyton Randolph, George Washington, Patrick Henry, Richard Bland, Benjamin Harrison, and Edmund Pendleton. Alas! where *now* shall we look for such names? The committees proceeded to organize and form them-

selves and their constituents into a unit. **They**
unanimously elected as their president the oldest
man, and from the oldest colony, Peyton Randolph.
(P. 893.) Now they are *one body*, and as *a body*
transacted much business in little time and with
amazing unanimity, for it had one spirit and one
life. It passed resolutions ; it discussed the interest of the country ; it adopted and signed articles
of association pledging abstinence from the use of
goods, "the growth, produce, and manufacture of
Great Britain ;" it published a bill of rights ; an
address "to the people of Great Britain ;" one "to
the inhabitants of these colonies ;" one "to the
inhabitants of the province of Quebec," in which
they urge them to *unite* their destinies with their
own. "In order to complete this highly desirable
union, they say, we submit it to your consideration,
whether it may not be expedient for you to elect
deputies to represent your province in the Continental Congress to be held at *Philadelphia* on the
10th day of May, 1775." (See Amer. Arch., 4th
series, vol. ii, p. 1819.)

There is an incident mentioned in a note at the
bottom of the page, in which was displayed the
spirit of liberal hospitality that to-day character-
ises the birthplace of independence and the home
of freedom. A few days after this unparalleled

band of sages constituted " the United Colonies,"
as they called themselves, an elegant dinner was
given by the friends of the great cause : a series of
toasts was prepared and drunk ; the fifth is in these
notable words : " PERPETUAL UNION TO THE COL-
ONIES."

On the 10th of May, 1775, " the Continental
Congress," this grand committee of the colonies,
again assembled in the same place, and elected the
same president. From their acts let us proceed in
the evidence of unity. We have already seen them
constitute what Kant would call " the unity of the
diverse," and neither they nor any others conceived
or viewed them in any other light than that of a
unit—the United Colonies in Congress assembled.
No body of men ever did or ever could feel themselves more perfectly united—more truly *one*. As
a grand committee of the colonies they met : they
organized by the appointment of all officers usual
and necessary for aggregate masses met for delibe-
ration. They transacted business in the name and
by the authority of the colonies united. Not a few
people, stuck on to the side of a barbarous continent,
only looked on and took an interest in their deliberations and decisions. The British king and people, France, the civilized world, stood in mute as-
tonishment—Humanity held its breath, and Liberty

trembled and sighed for the results. Such a body of men she had not before seen assembled in her cause. She had hovered over the Amphictyonic hall and listened to the last thrilling eloquence of Greece's most illustrious orator ; she had given an attentive ear to the silvery tones of Rome's most illustrious orator ; but never did she look in upon the deliberations of any assembly with more intense interest than when, on the 15th of June, 1775, the United Colonies in congress assembled passed the resolution, " That a General be appointed to command all the continental forces raised, and to be raised, for the defence of American liberty.

" That five hundred dollars per month be allowed for his pay and expenses."

" The Congress then proceeded to the choice of a General, when *George Washington*, Esq., was unanimously elected."

Nor did she abate a hair of her high hopes, when, next day, upon the announcement, by the president of this august body, being made to him of his appointment, the General elect delivered the following speech :

" Mr. President : Though I am truly sensible of the high honor done me in the appointment, yet I feel great distress, from a consciousness that my abilities and military experience may not be equal to the extensive and important trust. However, as the Congress desire it, I will enter upon the momentous duty, and exert every power I possess in their service and for the support of the glorious cause. I beg they will accept my most cordial thanks for this distinguished test of their approbation.

" But lest some unlucky event should happen, unfavorable to my reputation, I beg it may be remembered, by every gentleman in the room, that I this day declare, with the utmost sincerity, I do not consider myself equal to the command I am honored with.

" As to pay, sir, I beg leave to assure the Congress, that as no pecuniary consideration could have tempted me to accept this arduous employment, at the expense of domestic ease and happiness, I do not wish to make any profit from it. I will keep an exact account of my expenses. These, I doubt not, they will discharge, and that is all I desire." (P. 1848.)

Oh ! what a contrast this forms with many who are now in similar employment in our country. Look at the modesty, and even diffidence, and bring it up alongside of the boldness and self-sufficiency which continually present themselves. We have men by hundreds, almost by thousands, who feel delightfully assured and conscious that their abilities, military experience (present, but rather prospective), are fully equal to the command they wish to be honored with. Then again, look at the self-sacrifice and entire disinterestedness that refuses all pecuniary compensation and reward! and contrast it with the thousand speculators in the material of war and in the commissions required to use or destroy them.

But we may not turn aside from our line of march in pursuit of evidence of unity. The next step carries us forward but a single day. On the 17th of June, 1775, and at the very hour when the blood of Warren and his illustrious fellow heroes was baptizing Bunker Hill to freedom's cause, the commission was adopted and handed to the General-in-Chief. I need not copy the whole. Thus on the record it begins and ends—viz. : " The Delegates of the United Colonies of New Hampshire," &c., &c.

" *To George Washington, Esquire:* We, reposing special trust in your patriotism, valor, conduct, and fidelity, do, by these presents, constitute and appoint you to be General and Commander-in-Chief of the Army of the United Colonies," &c.

And in the last paragraph, they instruct him to regulate all his conduct and " follow such orders and directions, from time to time, as you shall receive from this or a future Congress of the United Colonies, or committee of Congress."

Thus, three times in Washington's commission, do they affirm the existence of the Union.

Let us see what evidence of its union preëxistent is contained in the Declaration. They were known as the United Colonies by England herself, and by the world, anterior to their own declaration of nationality, and to its recognition by any of the nations ; and thus it continued up to July 4, 1776, when they changed their name, not by rejecting the term *united*, but by rejecting *Colonies* and inserting *States*.

Here let me say, it is eminently due to truth and right to insist upon the fact that, until this point of time, no colony was a sovereign power— none put in the claim to be a sovereign power. Every colony acknowledged fealty to the British crown. The very name by which each denominated itself, by which the relation between them and Britain was habitually designated, and by which every nation on the globe recognized them — the very name by which the immortal Declaration itself designates them—the name *colony*—testifies that they were not sovereign powers. An association of men, in a colonial condition, may have, indeed must

4*

have and exercise many of the rights, privileges, and powers which are comprehended under the idea of sovereignty ; but some, and those the higher attributes of sovereignty, they cannot have. To be a *colony*, and to be a *sovereign power*, are contradictories, and can never agree. Try the combination, and see whether it be not only absurd in the very expression, but ridiculous. *A sovereign colony ! !*

The unity for which we contend is assumed in the very first sentence of the Declaration : " When, in the course of human events, it becomes necessary for one people to dissolve the political bonds which have connected them with another, and to assume among the powers of the earth the separate and equal station," &c. Here, demonstratively evident it is, that the colonies are a unit in this action—" ONE PEOPLE,"—and, moreover, that hitherto they were not—none of them even—not one of them was a sovereign power—not one of them had ever assumed among the powers of the earth a separate and equal station.

We proceed to the Declaration proper : " We, therefore, the representatives of the UNITED STATES OF AMERICA, in GENERAL CONGRESS assembled, appealing to the SUPREME JUDGE of the world for the rectitude of our intentions, do, in the name and by the authority of the good people of these colonies, solemnly publish and declare, that these United Colonies are, and of right ought to be, *free and independent States;* that they are absolved from all allegiance to the British crown, and that all political connection between them and the state of Great Britain, is and ought to be totally dissolved; and that, as FREE AND INDEPENDENT STATES, they have full power to levy war, conclude peace, contract alliances, establish commerce, and to do all other acts and things which INDEPENDENT STATES may of right do. And, for the support of this declaration, with a firm reliance upon the protection of DIVINE PROVIDENCE, we mutually pledge to each other our lives, our fortunes, and our sacred honor."

This most illustrious document is known the world over as the *Declaration of Independence,* and the whole civilized world has long ago interpreted it for themselves. It is perhaps the simplest, the plainest, and most unsophisticated document in the world. Nevertheless, it can be—it has been, misconstrued, and perverted to purposes so foul as to make all humanity weep, and pandemonium exult. But let us honestly ask:

1st. Independence on what, is herein declared? All civilized humanity returns but one answer—

independence on "the state of Great Britain." "All political connection between them and the state of Great Britain is, and ought to be, totally dissolved."

2d. But who are thus independent? Those who make the declaration. "We, the representatives of the United States of America." Surely not the individual men; but the *representatives*.

Now a representative must represent some persons, and these persons are his principals—his constituents; and he acts for them and by their authority. The question then reverts, whom did they represent? by whose authority did they act? "In the name, and by the authority of the *good people* of these colonies." There it is, just as now in our Constitution: "We, the PEOPLE," but acting through our representatives. As in the Constitution, We, the People of the United States, do ordain and establish this constitution; so here, We, the PEOPLE, do make this declaration. In both, the *people* are taken collectively as a unit—"one people."

3d. But are not the colonies to be taken severally? Are they not the constituents of the representatives? Did not the colonial legislatures appoint the members to the Congress? This last case is true—they were appointed by the assemblies; but it does not hence follow that they do not represent the people and act by their authority, for they say they do. The colonies cannot be viewed severally, for the very terms of the Declaration assure us that they are the representatives, not of the colonies severally, but "of the United States, in general congress assembled"—jointly, as a unit. Besides, we have seen most abundantly that even when they first met, September 5, 1774, they declared themselves united, and acted all along as one body; and Mr. Madison says:

"I hold it for a fundamental point, that an individual independence of the States is utterly irreconcilable with the idea of an aggregate sovereignty." (See Mad. Papers, p. 631).

General C. C. Pinckney says (see Elliott's Debates, vol. iv, p. 301): "The separate independence and individual sovereignty of the several States were never thought of by the enlightened band of patriots who framed this Declaration [he had just quoted the declaratory clause above cited]; the several States are not even mentioned by name in any part of it,—as if it was intended to impress this maxim on America, that our freedom and independence arose from our Union, and that without it we could neither be free nor independent. Let us, then, consider all attempts to weaken this Union, by maintaining that each State is separately and individually independent, as a species of political heresy, which can never benefit us, but may bring on us the most serious distresses." What a prophetic insight this most noble of South Carolinians had into our system and the basis on which it rests ! "Most serious distresses"—alas ! how they hang as a cloud of blood upon the land, precipitated in a deluge by this "political heresy !"

And his noble compeer, Hon. Charles Pinckney, after remarking "that this is the best government that has ever yet been offered to the world," added that without public spirit, "the national Union must ever be destroyed by selfish views and private interest." "He said that, with respect to the Union, this can only be remedied by a strong government, which, while it collects its powers to a point, will prevent that spirit of disunion from which the most serious consequences are to be apprehended. He begged leave, for a moment, to examine what effect this spirit of disunion must have upon us, as we may be affected by a foreign enemy. It weakens the consistency of all public measures, so that no extensive scheme of thought can be carried into action, if its accomplishment demands any long continuance of time. It weakens not only the consistency, but the vigor and expedition of all public measures ; so that, while a divided people are con-

tending about the means of security or defence, a
united enemy may surprise and invade them.
These are the apparent consequences of disunion."
(See Elliott's Debates, iv, 261.)

How imminent this danger of disunion at the
present time !   How easy it will be for France and
England, when we shall have still further exhausted
ourselves by this war of disunion, to step in and
wind up the Republic, and partition it out among
the despots of the old world ; and thus put an end
to the troubles which the spirit of freedom from our
country has afforded to despotic power !   Ay !
and how highly probable it is that this purpose
lies at the foundation of their neutral policy ; a
neutral policy which is the most likely course they
could pursue to be successful, on the supposition—
which doubtless is the truth as to the monarchy
and the aristocracy—that their object was the destruction of free government from the earth.

Hon. Robert Barnwell expressed himself equally strong on the vital necessity of Union.   In re-
sponding to Mr. Lowndes, he alleged that his whole
course against the Constitution had "as the basis
of his objections, that the Eastern States entertained
the greatest aversion to those which lay to the
South, and would endeavor in every instance to
oppress them.   This idea he considered as founded

in prejudice, and unsupported by facts. To prove
this assertion, Mr. B. requested gentlemen for a
moment to turn their attention to the transactions
which the late war has engraved upon the memory
of every man. When the arm of oppression lay
heavy on us, were they not the first to arouse themselves? When the sword of civil discord was'
drawn, were they not the first in the field? When
war deluged our [their?] plains with blood, what
was their language? Did they demand the Southern troops to the defence of the North? No! Or,
when war floated to the South, did they withhold
their assistance? The answer was the same.
When we stood with the spirit, but weakness of
youth, they supported us with the vigor and prudence of age. When our country was subdued,
when our citizens submitted to superior power, it
was then these States evinced their attachment.
He (Mr. Barnwell) saw not a man [it was in the
South Carolina Legislature these things were said,
when the question of calling a convention to ratify
the United States Constitution was under discus-
sion]—He saw not a man who did not know that
the shackles of the South were broken asunder by
the arms of the North."

Gen. Pinckney had said a little before, p. 283,
in reply to the same Mr. Lowndes: "The honor-

able gentleman alleges that the Southern States are weak. I sincerely agree with him. We are so weak that by ourselves we could not form a union strong enough for the purpose of effectually protecting each other. Without union with the other States, South Carolina must soon fall. Is there any one among us so much a Quixote as to suppose that this State could long maintain her independence if she stood alone, or was only connected with the Southern States? I scarcely believe there is," &c.

Such were the sentiments of the great men of the South : alas ! have the blood and spirit of the revolutionary patriots evaporated entirely from their soil ?

Nor did the great men of Virginia come short of these South Carolina witnesses for the truth. In the debates of the convention on the United States Constitution, Gov. Randolph winds up a powerful speech, in reply to Mr. Henry, who displayed not the statesman but the demagogue throughout, thus : "I shall conclude with a few observations, which come from my heart. I have labored for the continuance of the Union—the rock of our salvation. I believe that, as sure as there is a God in heaven, our safety, our political happiness and existence, depend on the union of the States ; and that without this union, the people of this and the other States will undergo the unspeakable calamities which discord, faction, turbulence, war, and bloodshed have produced in other countries. The American spirit ought to be mixed with American pride to see the Union magnificently triumphant. Let that glorious pride, which once defied the British thunder, reanimate you again. Let it not be recorded of Americans, that, after having performed the most gallant exploits, after having overcome the most astonishing difficulties, and after having gained the admiration of the world by their incomparable valor and policy, they lost their acquired reputation, their national consequence and happiness, by their own indiscretion. Let no future historian inform posterity that they wanted wisdom and virtue to concur in any regular, efficient government. Should any writer, doomed to so disagreeable a task, feel the indignation of an honest historian, he would reprehend and criminate our folly with equal severity and justice. Catch the present moment, seize it with avidity and eagerness—for it may be lost, never to be regained! If the Union be now lost, I fear it will remain so forever. I believe gentlemen are sincere in their opposition, and actuated by pure motives; but, when I maturely weigh the advantages of the Union, and dreadful consequences of its dissolution; when I see safety on my right, and destruction on my left ; when I behold respectability and happiness acquired by the one, but annihilated by the other—I cannot hesitate to decide in favor of the former." (Elliott's Debates, iii, 85, 86.) And thus throughout, the great ones of the country, North and South, believed the Union preceded the Declaration, and formed its basis ; and, by consequence, was indispensable to our freedom and nationality.

But the most indubitable evidence, *a posteriori*, as it were, of the Declaration being based and founded in union—that the independence was not of one another, but only of the state of Great Britain—is found in the subsequent history. Had it been their intention to assert for each State independence of all and every other—had they not designed to assume and vindicate political independence and unlimited political sovereignty for the Union only, and not for the colonies severally—then assuredly we should have seen the States, each for itself, at once arrogating to themselves and exercising all the attributes of sovereignty which, in the Declaration, had been withdrawn from the British crown. Each State must " have full power to levy war, conclude peace, contract alliances, establish commerce, and to do all other acts and things which INDEPENDENT STATES may of right do."

But now, what is the fact, as it looms out from their whole history? Did any of the States assume the exercise of these powers, or claim the abstract right even so to do? We have seen how jealousy of local colonial rights displayed itself in the little colonies of Plymouth, Connecticut, and New Haven, when they, with Massachusetts, formed "the United Colonies of New England." And how much more must this spirit have displayed itself, had the thought ever been entertained that the Declaration made thirteen independent sovereignties — thirteen nations. No; it is preposterously absurd and untrue, that any one State supposed this to be the intent of the act of separation. No; the foundation corner-stone of independence is UNION. Without antecedent, and coexistent, and the firm faith in subsequent union, the idea of independence had never been entertained. No State ever declared independence. Ratify the act of July 4th, the people and States did oftentimes, as we do to-day in all our meetings; but a declaration of independence by a State, averring itself to be a sovereign power— this is unknown to history. What State ever declared war, contracted alliances, received or sent out ambassadors to other nations?

But again, similar irresistible evidence is deduced from the notable fact, that no foreign power ever recognized such State independent sovereignty. What nation ever sent an ambassador to the national government of Pennsylvania, Virginia, Massachusetts!! The thing is utterly unheard of— never was done—never could be done.

Yet, the higher attributes of sovereignty having been withdrawn, on the formal ground of forfeiture under the laws of God, on account of non-user and abuse, these did not fall to the ground and leave the people of America in a state of anarchy. The Great God, who rules the destiny of men and of nations, and who is trying His grand experiment of free government on this broad continent, has so adjusted His divine plan as to leave nothing to the whim or caprice, the folly or the madness of a few ambitious and misguided men. He knows how to overrule these human attributes for its furtherance; He maketh the wrath and other sinful passions of man to praise Him, and restraineth the remainder. It will be necessary, to a due appreciation of the Divine scheme, that we revert to the political state of the colonies preceding the Declaration; that we study to understand the true nature and position of the Continental Congress, and then those of the Constitutional Convention, and their work. These three in order.

CHAPTER VII.

POLITICAL CONDITION OF THE COLONIES WHEN THE DECLARATION WAS UTTERED.

In the chapter on Sovereignty (IV) we had occasion to say that only parts of it can be transferred from and by the people, where God has placed it. It is utterly impossible that any one man, or any one association of men, can attend to the minute and multitudinous affairs of a great people. Moses was overburdened by the weight of his duties as a ruler, supernaturally thrown upon him, and sustained as he was by supernatural powers. Seventy-two vice-presidents, additional to the elders that came out of Egypt, were appointed, to relieve him of parts of the sovereignty. Still, this was an inadequate distribution, and hundreds of subordinate officers were spread all over the ten thousands of Israel. Every one of these officers, by *consent*—indeed by formal *election* at first—of the people, exercised within his particular sphere a portion of the sovereign power of ruling or governing. Similar was the condition of things with us. When we approached the Red Sea of our bloody Revolution, our twelve tribes were not a loose rabble; but, like Israel, each tribe had its officers, adapted to all the details of business indispensable in so large a community. Legislative, executive, and judicial officers, for the management of all the lower exercises of sovereignty, were familiar to the people in every State. The crossing of our Red Sea, so far from suspending the exercise of all these lower functions of sovereignty, left the whole machinery in full operation, and even strengthened and confirmed it by a perpetual union.

Let us pause here a moment, for speculation and inquiry. What has ever been the grand difficulty in the government of large masses of mankind? Has it not been this very matter of managing the minute and innumerable details nearest to the people? As you descend from the vast generalities of a mighty power, you meet the infinite ramifications which are involved in the necessary divisions of society. You must divide the country into sections, states, departments, counties, townships, corporations, precincts, wards, families; and for all these you must have your appropriate officers, every one invested with a portion of the sovereignty. Now, it appears to me, here lies the difficulty in a vast empire, under one supreme head. This head may be wise as Solon and energetic as Cæsar; but no man is omniscient, no man omnipotent. Ahasuerus, with all the wisdom of his seven chamberlains, failed in securing honest and faithful and efficient agents to manage his government, "from India to Ethiopia, over a hundred and seven and twenty provinces." No one heart has power to drive the current of political life through the distant members of so extended a body politic. It must stagnate at the extremities, and ultimately convey its corruption back to the centre. The empire of Xerxes, like his army, fell to pieces by its expansion. Alexander's dominion could not be sustained by one head, and perished with him. Rome conquered herself into fragments and fell to pieces, because she spread too wide for the practicability of a single government. Revolutionary, republican France—once Cæsar's province—now mighty as old Rome herself—split to pieces upon the rock of consolidation—"one and indivisible." With the *e pluribus unum* of the great western republic waving its peaceful folds within her view, she, nevertheless, never learned its grand lesson until too late. She attempted to govern France by one representative head, and failed. To the United States alone has the Ruler of the world revealed the great and priceless mystery of one general government, for the conduct of great national and international affairs, resting upon the broad and firm basis of the people of thirteen governments, appropriately adapted to conduct and care for all local and, as it were, domestic interests. This, I say, is God's revelation to America, and to the world through her. It is a *revelation*, not oral nor written on vellum, but providential. It is not the product of human genius. No man studied it out ; no man planned it. Neither the Prince of Condé nor Admiral Coligni ; neither John Smith nor John Robinson ; neither Gustavus Adolphus nor Henry IV.; neither Stuart nor Guelph ; neither Penn nor Oglethorpe— none of these, nor all combined, originated the grand conception. In the word of God, His people had found the representative principle—basis of democratic liberty—and in His providence guided, unconsciously to themselves, they, in the progress of two hundred years, worked out the grand problem of free government, and painted it, with their own blood, on the blue and the white, amid the stars of glory—E PLURIBUS UNUM ; and there let it shine, in the simplicity of its own grandeur, as long as a glimmering ray descends from the galaxy of heaven.

5

The colonies, at the date of independence, were distinct governments, in the constant exercise of a large and important part of sovereign powers, viz., those which lie nearest the homes of the people— local, domestic affairs, whose range went not beyond colonial bounds ; whilst as to exterior affairs and the relations they sustained to other colonies and to foreign nations—in other words, as to all that part of the sovereignty which had been hitherto vested in and exercised by the British Government, the States were not sovereign ; but had placed these powers in the hands of their own agents, the Continental Congress.

CHAPTER VIII.

THE CONTINENTAL CONGRESS.

THE most obvious remark on this body is, that it is *provisional*—it is intrusted with the temporary exercise of great powers, by an irregularity not susceptible of reduction—at least not susceptible of being easily and speedily reduced to regular and systematic form. This Congress is the residuary legatee of a defunct sovereign ; in trust, however, for the use of an insulted and injured people. The higher powers of sovereignty which were held by the crown, with consent of the colonies as far up as 1776, now reverted to the people ; yet not to them directly, but to the hands of the Congress, previously appointed as their agents to receive and exercise the same. These powers, it is well to repeat, returned to the people in consequence of their forfeiture by the crown. The right to rule is derived to the sovereign from God, through the people ; who, constrained by the tyrannical abuse of power, had appealed to the Supreme Ruler of the universe for its return to them, that they might vest it in the hands of their trusty friends, who thus became "the United States in Congress assembled."

This provisional or temporary agency, from the necessity of the case, must exercise a large discretion in fulfilment of their trust. Such a transition state, including the conduct of a seven years' war, cannot reasonably be looked to for examples of accurate conformity with the technical rules of law and the forms of an organized government. Substantial justice, indeed, their trust and their character authorize us to expect ; but defects and irregularities must not surprise us.

Hence my second general remark, that the Continental Congress were not, properly speaking, a government, but a temporary substitute in the absence of a government. The analysis given in our Constitution is true and exhaustive : government is resolved into three elements—the legislative, the executive, and the judiciary ; but now we find neither of these in its proper fulness of idea in the Congress.

Not the legislative ; for, though they deliberated with consummate wisdom, and decided with judgment clear and generally sound—though they passed resolutions and acts innumerable, in the nature of laws and even the forms, yet they lacked the grand element of legislation ; they had no power to enforce their laws, which, therefore, degenerated into simple counsel or advice. If they planned a campaign, decreed the levying of a body of troops and of the material and sinews of war, and struck the proportion or quotas which each State ought to furnish, still it depended on the good pleasure of the States whether their decrees would be carried out.

As is implied in the preceding paragraph, there was no executive head ; no civil officer endued with power and bound to see to the execution of the laws. Officers of the house, or special committees for the time being, filled up this gap.

Nor was there any semblance of any organized judiciary. Justice was administered through State authorities, and occasionally by committees ; and within its precincts, by military authority and agency. But for a body of law officers, devoted to the high and most important duty of holding courts and administering justice, we search in vain.

At best it was a *quasi* government ; or, to speak more correctly, we remark, thirdly, that this Congress was a grand committee of the States. So Massachusetts calls the members whom she recommends (see *ante*, p. 74) " a meeting of committees from the several colonies." So the Easton resolution, "a general congress of committees" (p. 75, *ante*). It was the age of committees; they had committees of vigilance, committees of safety, &c. But what is a committee? A select and small number of persons, appointed by a deliberative body to investigate some special subject and report to the body for their final action. It is of the nature of an inquest, and is sometimes, yet rarely, clothed with executive powers. Thus was it, to a great extent, with Congress. Their legislation was subject to revision by the State Legislatures. The practical working of the system—if system it might be called—shows the extreme jealousy of the people in reference to the higher functions of sovereignty. The abuses of them by the government at "home," as the Plan of Union calls the crown authorities, made them very cautious how they intrusted them even to their own committees; and hence they reserved the right to recall members at pleasure, and to appoint others.

CHAPTER IX.

THE ARTICLES OF CONFEDERATION AND PERPETUAL UNION.

ON the 11th day of June, 1776, a committee was appointed "for preparing the Declaration," and the next entry on the record is: "Resolved, that a committee be appointed to prepare and digest the form of a confederation to be entered into between these colonies." On the next day this was done by taking one member from each colony. This committee reported on the 12th of July, when eighty copies were ordered to be printed, the printer being put under oath of secrecy, and the members and officers under solemn injunction not to divulge the matter. The articles were taken up on the 22d of July in Committee of the Whole, and discussed on that day, and on ten other days, until Aug. 8, when the House gave leave to sit again "to-morrow." But the immense crowd of business, in vast detail, seems to have shoved the matter entirely out of sight, until April 2, 1777, when it was made an order for "Monday next, and that two days in the week be employed on that subject, until it shall be wholly discussed in Congress." But it seems to have been overlaid until Monday, April 21, when, after discussion, it was "postponed to Friday next." On May 5 it was again discussed, and then "postponed;" and between that date and Nov. 17, when, after some discussion of amendment, it was adopted finally, there were at least twenty-two days on which it was discussed, besides several when it was only taken up and postponed. This historical detail is presented, in order to impress the reader's mind with the magnitude of the work and the immense difficulties that lay in its way. Think of the character of the men, for intelligence, integrity, business tact, and earnestness, and that even these patriots spent from June 11, 1776, until Nov. 17, 1777, and for thirty-three different times discussed the matter and form of these ARTICLES OF CONFEDERATION AND PERPETUAL UNION, and you will readily infer it was no light task they had before them, and that it was no extravagant utterance of Judge William Henry Drayton, when, entering on the same discussion in the Legislature of South Carolina, he said : "God has called us forth to legislate for the new world, and to endeavor to bind the various people of it in durable bands of friendship and union."

The first thing which any intelligent reader will observe upon the face of this document is, that its leading object, its prominent and main design, is UNION. This he will see from its history. Independence of England, and mutual dependence on one another, stand asserted in adjoining lines. The printer can bring them no closer together. The same stroke that cuts us loose from our cruel mother, binds us together. The same blow that prostrates the sovereign on account of powers abused and forfeited, provides a deposit for these powers in safer hands.

Moreover, look at the phraseology—the very name and style of the paper force this upon you, as the master thought: "ARTICLES OF CONFEDERATION AND PERPETUAL UNION." This phrase, *perpetual union*, occurs in the document six times— "and the union shall be perpetual"; "the union shall be perpetual." "The United States in Congress assembled" occurs twenty-eight times; "the United States," twenty-seven times additional. But this enchanting union is not the final cause; it is a means to an end: Liberty is the grand end—defence, security, welfare, all included in liberty— these are the end; union is an indispensable means.

But this union is *federative*. "The style of

5*

this *confederacy* shall be, THE UNITED STATES OF AMERICA." The word CONFEDERATION occurs twelve times. It creates "a firm league of friendship." Now a league is a covenant between States, which changes not their organization, but simply pledges unity of action — coöperation in reference to the accomplishment of some particular object interesting to the parties contracting. This object is specified in Article III, and is nothing but the object already pursued by Congress. The league is nothing new, but is simply a formal expression of existent relations, duties, and obligations. Observe the phraseology: "Each State retains its sovereignty, freedom, and independence, and every power, jurisdiction, and right which is not by this confederation *expressly* delegated to the United States in Congress assembled." I have emphasized *expressly,* as indicating the previous and present *implied* exercise of certain powers by Congress. And the word *severally,* in Article III, shows that the States, as *States,* formed this league. They retain all the sovereignty, freedom, independence, &c., which they do not delegate; that is, when they proceed, as in Article IX, to define them—peace and war, sending and receiving ambassadors, entering into treaties and alliances, regulating the alloy and value of coin, fixing the

standard of weights and measures, trade with Indians, regulating post offices, &c.,—which are the
very parts and portions of the sovereignty they had
withdrawn from the crown and vested in Congress,
and which this body had been exercising ever since
June, 1775. Never did the States suppose their
sovereignty was any other or more extensive than
they had held it all along, when they were colonies. Nor, that their independence was anything
different from what they asserted in the Declaration, and had been enjoying ever since; for, in the
very confederation, or *act of covenanting together*
(which is the simple English of that Latin word),
they proclaim their dependence on each other.

The phrase, *The United States in Congress assembled*, which, as stated above, occurs twenty-
eight times, proves the same thing. It is the
States that assembled in Congress; the *States* that
vote separately as a unit—the *States*, severally as
individuals, but being assembled, the diversity is
merged in the unity.

Again, we remark, " The Articles of Confederation and Perpetual Union " are designed to assert
the perpetuity of the union, not of the articles.
For Article XIII, which affirms " the union shall
be perpetual," also makes provision for alterations,
if " agreed to in a Congress of the United States,

and be afterwards confirmed by the Legislature of every State." The whole people felt the necessity of it, and dreaded dissolution as the greatest possible calamity.

And lastly here, the articles do not create a government, but leave everything, almost, precisely as before their adoption. Governing power they recognize in Congress; the higher functions of sovereignty are conceded, and in many respects regulated; but analyzed and distributed into the three departments, under appropriate officers, these powers are not. All that has just been said in Chapter VIII of the Congress before, is applicable to them after the adoption of the articles. They provide no *legislative*, no *executive*, no *judiciary*, in any full and proper sense of those terms. They are simply an authoritative letter of instruction to the Congress, as the Grand Committee of the States.

This scheme of union was resisted in many of the State Legislatures, and on various grounds, which caused much delay. It was not until March 1, 1781, that Maryland, the last to do it, acceded, and on the next day Congress met under the articles.

CHAPTER X.

THE CONSTITUTION:

ITS OCCASION—ITS FIRST OBJECT, UNION—A GOVERNMENT
SUPPORTED BY SOUTHERN VOTES.

No man who reads the minutes of the Continental Congress, before and after the adoption of the articles, and marks the multiplicity and variety of business they were called to perform, can for a moment wonder at the impracticability of that system of administration. Whilst the superincumbent weight of the revolutionary struggle lay upon the arch federal, it was held together ; but, this removed by the peace of '83, the centrifugal force rapidly tended to and foreboded ruin. This grand committee created by the States was felt by them to be almost powerless. Congress is our creature—they seem to have reasoned—our servant, and our obedience to our servant is optional. Hence feebleness. But worse than this. The articles left the imposition of duties on imports in the hands of the States. Of course, the State which levied the lightest duty would draw the trade to her ports. Difficulties soon sprung up. Virginia and Maryland interfered with each other, and ill blood was stirred. Attempts were made to adjust the matter, but in vain. Congress also failed to raise a revenue to meet necessary means to defray the expenses of government and pay the public debt. Credit began to break down. Anarchy threatened to produce a ruin which the power of England failed to bring about. The patriot heart began to tremble for the ark of safety. In a letter to James Madison, from R. H. Lee, then President of Congress, dated the 26th of November, 1784, he says : " It is by many here suggested as a very necessary step for Congress to take, the calling on the States to form a convention for the sole purpose of revising the Confederation, so far as to enable Congress to execute with more energy, effect, and vigor the powers assigned to it, than it appears by experience that they can do under the present state of things." The answer of Mr. Madison remarks : " I hold it for a maxim, that the union of the States is essential to their safety against foreign danger and internal contention ; and that the perpetuity and efficacy of the present system cannot be confided in. The question, therefore, is, in what mode, and at what moment, the experiment for supplying the

defects ought to be made." Mad. Papers, p. 707-8.
This sentiment soon became general with leading
men all over the Union, and led to the Convention.
"As a natural consequence of this distracted and
disheartening condition of the Union, the Federal
authority had ceased to be respected abroad, and
dispositions were shown there, particularly in Great
Britain, to take advantage of its imbecility, and to
speculate on its approaching downfall. At home
it had lost all confidence and credit." "It was
known that there were individuals who had be-
trayed a bias toward monarchy, and there had
always been some not unfavorable to a partition of
the Union into several confederacies; either from a
better chance of figuring on a sectional theatre, or
that the sections would require stronger governments, or by their hostile conflicts lead to a monarchical consolidation. The idea of dismemberment had recently made its appearance in the
newspapers."

"Such were the defects, the deformities, the dis-
eases and the ominous prospects for which the convention were to provide a remedy, and which ought
never to be overlooked in expounding and appreci-
ating the constitutional charter, the remedy that
was provided." (P. 713, 714.)

On all hands it was and is admitted that the

Federal Government, so called, was too weak to sustain life for any length of time. It lacked power and energy, or, as I hold, was not a government at all, in any just sense of that term, but only a Grand Committee of the States.

Such being the situation of the country, let me ask the reader, what do you think will be the prime, leading, grand object before the minds of this most illustrious body ? What the pole-star to guide them through the rocks and quicksands of this sea of anarchy ? Who, that hath a soul tremblingly alive for the cause of free government and the hopes of humanity, does not at once respond, UNION—the glorious thirteen in ONE : E PLURIBUS UNUM ? And what say the *convention* themselves? Their response meets you in the forefront of the Constitution : " We, the people of the United States, in order to form a more perfect Union," &c. The preamble sets forth the grand design of the law ; and here it is, first, the formation of a more perfect Union—more perfect than what ? Certainly, more perfect than existed before under the articles. But these affirm, repeatedly, *the Union shall be perpetual*. This is the leading, the felt necessity. Then it meets you at the close. Read it, in the letter submitting their finished work to the Congress. " In all our deliberations on this subject, we

kept steadily in our view that which appears to us
the greatest interest of every true American—the
consolidation of our UNION—in which is involved
our prosperity, felicity, safety, perhaps our national
existence. This important consideration, seriously
and deeply impressed on our minds, led each State
in the convention to be less rigid on points of inferior magnitude than might have been otherwise
expected ; and thus the Constitution which we now
present is the result of a spirit of amity and of that
mutual deference and concession which the peculi-
arity of our political situation rendered indispensable."

To this last remark permit me to call attention
for a moment. These profoundly wise and patriotic
men—this more than Roman Senate or Amphictyonic council—acknowledge themselves hemmed in
and shut up, and providentially constrained to act
and do precisely as they did—it was *indispensable.*
And this is what I mean, when I affirm this consti-
tion to be the most stupendous fabric ever erected
by human genius ; yea, a *quasi* inspired production.
No man ever planned such a government as ours.
On the contrary, it was long held that an *imperium
in imperio* was a contradiction, an impossibility, an
absurdity ; but Divine Providence superintended
this whole movement, and led our fathers to the

construction of a system unknown hitherto in the history of the human race—a plan of union and of separation affording the largest freedom and securing the most energetic operation of power—a system where law is sovereign—law abiding in the individual conscience and spreading itself over the entire surface of society, securing the greatest happiness to the largest number.

But it has been already admitted, that even Union, the first object of these patriots, was a means to an end. The prosperity, felicity, safety, national existence, are involved in it, for these depend upon their success in establishing a government. After the election, by unanimous ballot, of George Washington as the president of the convention, and the arrangement of a few small matters, the very first principle they decided was, that a government should be formed. Edmund Randolph presented fifteen resolutions, which constituted the basis of their action, the third of which was the first adopted in committee, after amendment, in these words, viz., " Resolved, that it is the opinion of this committee that a national government ought to be established, consisting of a supreme legislature, executive, and judiciary."

Accordingly the constitution contains the exhaustive analysis of government into the three elements, legislative, executive, and judiciary. In this there is a strong contrast to the articles of confederation, which, as we have seen (Chap. IX), establishes neither of the three. This settled the question of a mere confederacy or confederation. The word confederation occurs in the articles twelve times and confederacy once ; but in the Constitution it occurs but twice, viz., art. i, sec. 10 : "No State shall enter into any treaty, alliance, or confederation ;" and art. vi, 1 : "All debts shall be as valid as under the confederation." Now why this studied exclusion of the very term ; it is never applied at all to the Constitution, but the word *constitution* is given as the very name of the new document, and is used in the body of it a dozen of times. It is moreover noticeable that the word constitution never occurs at all in the old articles. I say, why are these things so ? Is it not designed thereby to show the entire difference of the two papers ? The one designates it a confederacy or league between the States, but does not create a government, and of course does not furnish a constitution, or elementary platform of fundamental law ; but the other writes out a system of such law and calls it "this CONSTITUTION."

The articles were adopted by the States as such ; the Constitution by the people, "We, the

PEOPLE, do ordain and establish this *constitution*." Here we have the theory of democratic republican government exemplified. The power of ruling is vested by his Creator in man; and man designates the agency for its exercise. Thus the theory of a mere confederation of States is carefully excluded.

The same is set forth in the letter of the convention to the president of Congress, accompanying the Constitution. It clearly and explicitly repudiates the idea of entire State independence.

" The friends of our country have long seen and desired that the power of making war, peace, and treaties; that of levying money and regulating commerce; and the correspondent executive and judiciary authorities should be fully and effectually vested in the general government of the Union; but the impropriety of delegating such extensive trust to one body of men is evident : hence results the necessity of a different organization."

" It is obviously impracticable, in the Federal government of these States, to secure all rights of independent sovereignty to each, and yet provide for the interest and safety of all."

It would be difficult to express the idea more explicitly of a limited State sovereignty, unless we adopt the language of the old articles : " ii. Each State retains its sovereignty, freedom, and independence, and every power, jurisdiction, and right which is not by this confederation expressly delegated to the United States in Congress assembled." Here is clearly set forth a restricted, a limited, a partial sovereignty, freedom, and independence, as belonging to the States as States. Nor is the same less distinctly uttered in the Constitution itself. Art. vii, 2 : " This constitution and the laws of the United States which shall be made in pursuance thereof ; — — shall be the supreme law of the land,—anything in the constitution or laws of any State to the contrary notwithstanding."

The same is proved by the very jealousy which produced the 10th article, in amendments. " The powers not delegated to the United States by the Constitution, nor prohibited by it to the States, are reserved to the States respectively, or to the people."

Indubitably the States are not absolutely sovereign under the Constitution ; they were sovereign only in a limited sense, and not absolutely, under the articles of confederation and perpetual union ; and they never were, even before, sovereignties absolute, as we have seen, chap. vii, but had created a body politic, as the trustee of the higher powers of sovereignty held by the crown, before they withdrew them from the royal trustee ; and, as before stated, the representatives of the United States made this

withdrawal " in the name, and by the authority of
the GOOD PEOPLE of these colonies."

And yet, with such facts staring him in the
face, Mr. Jefferson Davis, in his message in May,
1861, denounces as a monstrous thing, " the rise
and growth in the Northern States of a political
school which has persistently claimed that the government thus formed was not a compact between
States, but was in effect a National Government,
set above and over the States." But let us ask
Mr. Davis whence this party for a National Government had its rise. The Madison Papers assure
us it had a Southern origin. Mr. Edmund Randolph uses the phrase *National Legislature*, in his
fifteen resolutions, twelve times. His seventh resolution says, " that a national executive be instituted "; and his ninth, " that a national judiciary
be established." Mr. Madison strenuously advocated a National Government. He says (see Mad.
Papers, p. 632) : " Let the National Government
be armed with a positive and complete authority in
all cases where uniform measures are necessary; as
in trade," &c., &c.

" Let it have a negation in all cases whatsoever, on the legislative action of the States, as the
King of Great Britain heretofore had. This I conceive to be essential, and the best possible abridg-
ment of the State sovereignties.

" Let this national supremacy be extended also to the judicial department.

" A Government formed of such extensive powers ought to be well organized. A national executive will also be necessary."

Colonel George Mason, of Virginia, strongly advocated a National Government. " He took this occasion to repeat, that, notwithstanding his solicitude to establish a National Government, he never would agree to abolish the State Governments, or render them absolutely inefficient." Ib., p. 910–12.

Charles Pinckney, South Carolina, presented a " Plan of a Federal Constitution," at least as strong as that adopted. Ib., p. 735.

Charles Cotesworth Pinckney, South Carolina, offered a resolution for " a more effective Government, consisting of a legislative, executive, and judiciary." P. 749. He " thought the second branch [the Senate] ought to be permanent and independent." P. 819. In short, it is indubitably true, that a strong National Government was advocated in Convention mainly by the Southern members ; all the leading Southern men having taken a decided stand in support of it, whilst the opposition to a National Government was chiefly from the North. Mr. Ellsworth, of Connecticut, moved, and Mr. Graham, of Massachusetts, seconded the motion, to strike out the word *national* from Mr. Randolph's resolution. P. 908. Mr. Patterson, of New Jersey, proposed a plan for enlarging the powers of Congress, but not for creating, properly speaking, a National Government. His was designated in the convention as the "*federal* plan," in contradistinction from "a national plan." Mr. Gouverneur Morris, Pennsylvania, explained the distinction between a *federal* and a *national, supreme* Government; the former being a mere compact resting on the good faith of the parties, the latter having a complete and *compulsive* operation. He contended that in all communities there must be one supreme power, and only one." Mad. Papers, p. 748.

"Mr. Wilson, Pennsylvania, entered into a contrast of the principal points of the two plans, so far, he said, as there has been time to examine the one last proposed. These points were: 1. In the Virginia plan there are two, and in some degree three, branches in the Legislature; in the plan from New Jersey there is to be a *single* Legislature only. 2. Representation of the people at large is the basis of the one; the State Legislatures the pillars of the other. 3. Proportional representation prevails in one, equality of suffrage in the other. 4. A single executive magistrate is at the head of the one ; a plurality is held out in the other. 5. In the one, a majority of the people of the United States must prevail ; in the other, a minority may prevail. 6. The National Legislature is to make laws in all cases to which the separate States are incompetent, &c.; in place of this, Congress are to have additional power in a few cases only. 7. A negative on the laws of the States ; in place of this, coercion to be substituted. 8. The executive to be removable on impeachment and conviction, in one plan ; in the other, to be removable at the instance of a majority of the executives of the States. 9. The revision of the laws provided for in one ; no such check in the other. 10. Inferior national tribunals in one ; none such in the other. 11. In the one, jurisdiction of national tribunals to extend, &c.; an appellate jurisdiction only allowed to the other. 12. Here, the jurisdiction is to extend to all cases affecting the national peace and harmony ; there, a few cases only are marked out. 13 Finally, the ratification is, in this, to be by the people themselves ; in that, by the Legislative authorities, according to the thirteenth article of the Confederation."

Now, if we consider that, on the vote between these two plans, there were but three negatives, and Maryland divided, and that Virginia, North Caro-

lina, South Carolina, and Georgia voted for Mr.
Randolph's plan, it excites our wonder to see Mr.
Jeff. Davis assert that this school, which went in
for a national government, had its rise and growth
in the Northern States. (See Mad. Papers, p. 904.)
Is there no regard to be paid to historical truth ?

Additional proof that the Constitution was
adopted, not by the States as sovereign powers, but
by the *people*, is found in the fact, that this very
point was raised in his first speech in the Virginia
convention by Mr. Henry, the most bitter and in-
veterate opponent of the Constitution. " I am sure
they were fully impressed with the necessity of
forming a great consolidated government, instead
of a confederation. That this [the Constitution] is
a consolidated government is demonstrably clear ;
and the danger of such a government is, to my
mind, very striking. I have the highest veneration
for those gentlemen ; but, sir, give me leave to demand, what right had they to say, *We, the people ?*
My political curiosity, exclusive of my anxious solicitude for the public welfare, leads me to ask, who
authorized them to speak the language of *We, the
people,* instead of *We, the State ?* States are the
characteristics and the soul of a confederation. If
the States be not the agents of this compact, it
must be one great, consolidated national govern-

ment of the people of all the States." (See Ell.
Deb., iv, 22.) True, Mr. Patrick Henry; and the
word "national," put in by his Excellency Governor
Randolph of Virginia, was stricken out on motion
of Mr. Ellsworth of Connecticut. True, Mr. Henry;
that is the very word put by the convention into
their letter accompanying the Constitution, which
letter was signed by one George Washington. "In
all our deliberations on this subject, we kept steadily
in our view that which appears to us the greatest
interest of every true American—the *consolidation*
of our Union—in which is involved our prosperity,
felicity, safety, perhaps our national existence."
Thus, on the third day of their sessions, Mr. Henry
raised the phantom demon of a consolidated national
government, and the ghostly spectre haunted him
to the end.

In response to the challenge of Mr. Henry, Gov.
Randolph says (p. 28), " The gentleman then proceeds, and inquires why we [the convention, of
which he was a leading member] assumed the language of 'We, the people?' I ask, why not?
The government is for the people; and the misfor-
tune was that the people had no agency in the government before. . . . . What harm is there in con-
sulting the people on the construction of a government by which they are to be bound? Is it un-

fair ? Is it unjust ? If the government is to be binding upon the people, are not the people the proper persons to examine its merits or defects ?"

Mr. Pendleton (p. 37) : " But an objection is made to the form ; the expression, 'We, the people,' is thought improper. Permit me to ask the gentleman who made this objection, who but the people can delegate powers ? Who but the people have a right to form government ? The expression is a common one, and a favorite one with me. The representatives of the people, by their authority, is a mode wholly inessential. If the objection be, that the Union ought to be one, not of the people, but of the State governments, then I think the choice of the former very happy and proper. What have the State governments to do with it ? Were they to determine, the people would not, in that case, be the judges upon what terms it was adopted."

It is prominent on the whole face of the debates, that the question between a confederacy and a strong national government was openly and distinctly controverted throughout, and on the final vote the Nationals had eighty-nine, and the Federals, *properly* so called, *i. e.*, those who went for a Confederate government, had seventy-nine. And it is well worthy of note, the adopting act runs:

"in the name and in behalf of the people of Virginia," not of the State or representatives ; and this stands in bold contrast with the action of the confederated secession constitution, which runs thus : " We, the deputies of the sovereign and independent States of South Carolina, &c., do hereby, in behalf of these States, ordain and establish this Constitution." Thus the people are ignored.

CHAPTER XI.

A PLAIN, unsophisticated man reads the Constitution, the history of its formation and adoption, and then is interrogated as to who adopted it : he feels no embarrassment, but tells you at once it was adopted by the people of the United States. He goes behind this, and assures you it was made by the people through their agents or representatives. Still farther, these representatives in the convention, acting for the people, were appointed to do this work by the Legislatures of the several States. Once more he tells you, the men who composed these different Legislatures were elected by the people in the several districts of their States respectively. He has a perfect understanding, in the concrete, of the whole subject. The people of each county or district choose a man to go up and legislate for the people of the State. The laws passed by this collective mass of individuals from the counties, are binding upon all the people, although the people in a given county did not vote but for one member. The legislators act for the people, the whole people. They are under bonds to seek the good of the whole. In the forming state, under the *provisional government*, the people's representatives in the State Legislatures respectively appointed certain citizens, each of their own State, to meet in a congress, as a kind of grand committee, to consult for the good of the whole colonies, now united in this very body. This congress, amid an infinitude of business which they transacted for the people, recommended the Legislatures of the States to appoint another set of men to meet and form a government for the whole people. This they did ; this congress was called a convention. Ask, now, this unsophisticated man : Whom did the members of this convention represent ?—for whom did they act ? His answer is prompt : For the people, whose representatives appointed them. But whom do you mean by the people ? Is it those of your county for which they act, and none else ? Is it for the people of your State, whose Legislature sent them to the convention ? or is it for the people spread over all the States ? His answer is—for the last, assuredly. They are the special representatives of the whole people of the United States, bound to consult the general good.

According to the response of this common-sense man, all is simple and plain; and so the production of the representatives of the whole people, in convention assembled, is submitted to the people for their acceptance or rejection. But, just as it is impracticable, and unsafe if practicable, for the whole population, or even the whole adult male population of a State, to meet in legislative council personally and pass laws; so it was impracticable, and unsafe if practicable, for the whole male population of the United States to meet in one grand legislative assembly and act on this constitution—this law of laws—this legislation that is to bind and limit all national legislation: *therefore* it must, by necessity, be submitted to the people of the States severally, through their representatives in convention assembled. It might, indeed, have been submitted to the State Legislatures; and this method had several advocates in the Convention. But the ratification by conventions in the States prevailed, as it kept the two Governments, State and National, separate.

If the people make their own laws, as is most meet, because God has placed the whole sovereignty in their hands, it is supremely fit and proper they should enact that fundamental law which is designed and destined to control future lawmakers.

This was done. "We, the people of the United States, * * * do ordain and establish this CONSTITUTION." There it stands on the record, and there it will stand forever. The people can govern themselves, but only by applying to themselves the everlasting truths of God's most holy law.

But now, if you sophisticate, you may puzzle our plain man. Ask him whether the people of each State acted as a State independent and sovereign, or as part of the greater people of the whole nation, and you force him into the fog of the great Southern abstractionist. Mr. Calhoun, in his celebrated speech on Jackson's Force Bill, says : "According to my conception, the whole sovereignty is in the several States, whilst the exercise of sovereign power is divided—a part being exercised under compact through this General Government, and the residue through the separate State Governments. But if the Senator from Virginia (Mr. Rives) means to assert that the twenty-four States form but one community, with a single sovereign power as to the objects of the Union, it will be but the revival of the old question of whether the Union is a union between States, as distinct communities, or a mere aggregate of the American people, as a mass of individuals ; and in this light his opinions would lead directly to consolidation."

C*

Now let our simple, honest denizen apply his powers to this statement, and see what he can make of it. But let us aid him, *if we can*. And, 1st remark: Are the several States in whom is the sovereign power to be taken as the people, being a mass of individuals, or is it the abstract conception of a government that is meant?

But, 2d. The whole sovereignty, he says, is in the several States; therefore, there being twenty-four whole States severally taken, there are twenty-four whole sovereignties!

But, 3d. Whilst the whole sovereignty is in the twenty-four States, i. e., twenty-four wholes, the exercise of sovereign power is divided—part being exercised by this General Government; i. e., the power is exercised where it is not! The whole is in the States; a part of that same whole is exercised by and in the United States Government!

4. Mr. Calhoun seems to deny that the twenty-four States form but one community; i. e., he denies that the people of the United States are united!—are "one people"—as in the Declaration.

5. He denies that the United States have a single sovereign power, even as to the *objects of the Union*—that they are sovereign within the limits of the Constitution.

6. He denies that the Constitution is designed

to consolidate the States ; whilst we have heard the
Convention affirm in their letter, "In all our deliberations on this subject, we kept steadily in our view
that which appears to us the greatest interest of
every true American—*the consolidation of our
Union.*" Then is Mr. Calhoun not a *true American*, in the eyes of Washington and his Convention ?   And so it proves this day : the blood of
thousands, of tens of thousands, is poured out, and
is now (September 20, 1862) running, as the necessary consequent of these wicked doctrines.   A vast
harvest of death succeeds this seedtime of abstract
nonsense and foggy philosophy.   Whereas, nothing
is more patent and better understood, or can be
more clearly expressed, than that the "one people," who published the Declaration in 1776, who
united together in the Continental Congress, did
also adopt the Constitution.   Every precaution was
taken to guard against the notion of a mere confederacy of States, and to make it clear and plain
that a Government was to be established by *the
people*—a Government superior to and above the
States separately considered, and as confederate
under the articles ; yet a Government restricted
and limited by lines clearly defining the bounds
between it and the State Governments—a Government, at whose formation this whole question of

State rights was most amply discussed on all sides, by *such men*—men who saw at a glance, as they say in their letter to Congress, "It is obviously impracticable, in the Federal Government of these States, to secure all rights of independent sovereignty to each, and yet provide for the interest and safety of all;" and who therefore adjusted the boundaries of each, and then submitted the whole to THE PEOPLE in conventions assembled. These supreme arbitrators, after long canvassing the matter of the Constitution, in their social meetings, in their popular movements toward the election of members for their several conventions, and then by their representatives in convention assembled, came to the grand conclusion, once more, that they form *one people*—one nation.

It seems almost trifling on a grave subject, when men allege the fact that the ratifying conventions were called by the State Legislatures, and met within the States severally, as evidence that the United States is merely a confederacy of independent States, and not "a National Government, set up above and over the States." To this, as an argument, the easy response is, that the *convenience* of submitting the ratification through the action of State Legislatures, was the governing idea. A second convention of the whole was proposed, but not seriously advocated. The language of George Mason, certainly one of the safest and wisest men in the Virginia delegation, is cogent, and worthy of serious consideration. " Colonel Mason considered a reference of the plan to the authority of the people, as one of the most important and essential of the resolutions. The Legislatures have no power to ratify it. They are the mere creatures of the State constitutions, and cannot be greater than their creators. And he knew of no power in any of the constitutions—he knew there was no power in some of them—that could be competent to this object. Whither then must we resort ? To the people, with whom all power remains that has not been given up in the constitutions derived from them. It was of great moment, he observed, that this doctrine should be cherished, as the basis of free government. Another strong reason was, that, admitting the Legislatures to have a competent authority, it would be wrong to refer the plan to them, because succeeding Legislatures, having equal authority, could undo the acts of their predecessors ; and the National Government would stand, in each State, on the weak and tottering foundation of an act of Assembly." (Mad. Papers, p. 1177.) These opinions were sanctioned by Mr. Madison (see Papers, 1183). The ratification, then, or adoption of the Constitution was by the people, not of Massachusetts or New York; not by the people of Pennsylvania, or Virginia, or South Carolina, as Mr. Jefferson Davis says; but WE, THE PEOPLE OF THE UNITED STATES."

CHAPTER XII.

THE CONSTITUTION NOT FEDERAL.

In our first chapter we endeavored to show that human society is not a *voluntary association*, in the usual sense of that phrase. Its existence did not originate in human volition, but in the divine. The whole theory of a *social compact* is utterly baseless—a mere speculation, without a single fact in man's history on which to rest. If it were a harmless theory, very well, let it pass. But it is a pernicious fancy, and has produced fearful fallacies and some of the most disastrous consequences. Some of these fallacies are now soaking our soil with the blood of its inhabitants. It is honestly believed, by many of our unhappy and misguided brethren of the South, that the United States Constitution is a *Federal Compact*, and creates a *Federal Government*. If the reader has embraced the doctrines of our first four chapters, we shall have little difficulty in exposing to his satisfaction and refuting this error.

And 1. Let us to the word : *Federal* is from the

Latin, *Fœdus*, meaning a *covenant* or *league*. The term *Federal*, therefore, implies the idea of a *covenant, agreement*, or *league* ; and, if applied to society, assumes as true the false doctrines exposed in our first chapter. But when applied to communities of men organized into states or governments, it imports some specific articles or matters about which the covenant is made. The nations—two or more there must be—agree ; they enter into a covenant, compact, treaty, for the accomplishment or security of some matter of interest to the contracting parties ; and this makes them *one, quoad hoc*, but not *one* as to anything outside of the specific terms of the contract. But, in the essential nature of a compact, it cannot be a government invested with the ordinary powers. Two nations may, indeed, contract to uphold, by recognition and by forces loaned, another people as a nation ; but they cannot possibly make a nation or establish a government out of themselves, comprehending themselves. They must, by necessity, merge their duality into a unity, and instead of the two becoming three, they become one.

True, two nations may appoint, by covenant, a joint commission, to exercise some political functions in their name and authority, but then, such is not a government, a new nation. So the Colonies acted through their grand committee. Such arrangement, however, cannot be permanent, but must eventuate in dissolution or in a government. Let the reader attempt to mature the conception of two governments covenanting to become one and yet remaining two, and he will soon convince himself of the absurdity of two or of thirteen supreme sovereign nations covenanting themselves into one sovereign nation—*i. e.*, the absurdity of the phrase *Federal Government.* Therefore,

2. The word *Federal* is nowhere found in our Constitution. Once only is it used in the letter ; but then, as the phrase *General Government* occurs in the immediately preceding sentence, evidently because the writer wished to avoid repetition, and used *Federal* as a synonym for *General.* Manifestly the idea in both cases is identical. Or it occurs in the letter in that loose and general sense which grew up under the old Articles. I contend that the absence of the word *Federal* from the Constitution is not accidental. Its use was redundant all over the land—in Congress, in the money market, in the mouths of all men everywhere ; in the Convention, in the public prints. Now, why is it entirely excluded from the Constitution ? Has this omission no significance ? Notoriously, the longest and hardest battle fought by those beloved and

loving friends of liberty, was just on this question, whether to adhere to the Federal system, or to adopt a National Government. When, therefore, the Virginia doctrine triumphed, and the Convention, by overwhelming majorities, determined to reject the mere confederation and to establish a General Government, they very properly repudiated and rejected the term *Federal ;* neither the name nor the thing can be found in the Constitution.

And yet, Mr. Jefferson Davis, who notices this omission, speaks thus : "The States endeavored in every possible form to exclude the idea that the separate and independent sovereignty of each State was merged into one government or nation ; and the earnest desire they evinced to impress on the Constitution its true character, that of a compact between independent States, the Constitution of 1787 having, however, omitted the clause already recited." Mr. Davis sees no evidence herein of any difference between the Articles and the Constitution ; this, he insists, is still merely a *compact ;* although the designed omission of every word expressive of that idea—*compact, covenant, federal, confederacy, confederation*—more than omission, the *exclusion* of every such term, stares him in the face ; yet all this affords this gentleman no proof at all against a confederacy and in favor of a government. The Constitution itself calls it a Government : Art. II.—" Seat of Government of the United States." The letter speaks of " the General Government." All nations recognize it as a Government ; Mr. Secretary and Mr. Senator Davis served it as a Government, and received his wages from his master—but alas ! all this availeth me nothing so long as I see Mordecai the [Black Republican] Jew sitting at the king's gate. The hundred and seven and twenty provinces from India to Ethiopia, are, after all, only "a compact."

But before this solemn ostracism of the word, it had passed into common currency, and became the name of a party, and of that party too who had expurgated both name and thing from the Constitution of the country. It was a most singular summerset. The Federal party they were called, who had repudiated federalism and established a national government as a counter system to it. We have in this an exemplification of the way in which the generic meaning of a word is entirely lost sight of, and it comes into use as a mere arbitrary appellative. By *Federal Government* is now meant nothing more than, or different from, *General* or *National Government*—simply to distinguish it from State Governments.

CHAPTER XIII.

FALLACY EXPLAINED—SYLLOGISM.

FALLACIES CHIEFLY RESULT FROM CREATING A FOURTH TERM.

WE are now in possession of the elements necessary for exposing the false logic that is desolating our country; but before proceeding, it will be proper, for the sake of such readers as are not familiar with the logical process, except in its unscientific forms, to give a brief chapter on Fallacy, the most important part of Logic. Yet, in order to show what Fallacy is and how to detect it, we must first have an idea of what an act of reasoning is : I apprize the unlearned reader that it is exceedingly simple—so simple that he will be ready to suppose I am trifling with him. The greatest of England's metaphysicians committed a great sin against humanity when he assailed the syllogism or formal statement of an argument, or act of reason. Its very simplicity, and a mistake of its true intent and proper use, led John Locke, in an evil and sad hour, to do against the syllogism such battle as has since covered many a field with blood.

Great men only can do great mischief—great reasoners only can become great sophists.

Logic is the art of reasoning, and the science of its principles ; and this is the actual order of their existence. Men reason now before they can give a reason for the process which they perform—before they can lay down a rule for it. So it was before the father of the technical syllogism was born. Aristotle's mother reasoned as soundly as he could do, after he wrote his logic. So men talk, and talk correctly, without understanding the grammar rules which they practice. So it is with most arts. The blacksmith welds the iron and tempers the steel, but understands not the chemical laws on which the process depends.

But we proceed :	A equals B,

C equals A,

Therefore,	C equals B.

My cane is as long as your umbrella,

His yardstick is as long as my cane,

Therefore, His yardstick is as long as your umbrella.

Or, negatively :	A does not agree with B,

C agrees with A,

Therefore,	C does not agree with B.

No traitor should command an army,

General Nemo is a traitor,

Therefore, General Nemo should not command an army.

This is the sum of the logical processes : vary and modify it the mind can; but go beyond these principles it cannot ; and the whole rests on the two simple axioms—Things which are equal to one and the same third thing, are equal to one another,— Two things, one of which agrees with one and the same third thing, and the other differs, differ from one another. The carpenter wants a piece of timber to reach from one wall to another ; he stretches his line from wall to wall ; then stretches the same line on the timber, and finds these agree, hence concludes this piece will answer his purpose. Here is an act of reasoning, and, if written in the logical formula above, it makes a syllogism. Now you perceive that there are three comparisons made here, and yet but three things compared. These things—the names of them—are called in logic *terms*, and each is used twice. The line and the distance of the walls are compared ; the same line and the length of the timber are compared. These are done mechanically and in the mind too ; and then, mentally only the timber and the distance of the walls are perceived to agree : this is the conclusion. Now, suppose the line to be elastic tape, could you compare these two lengths through the medium of such a line ? This would deceive you ; it would be a fallacious proof of their agreement ;

it would be a fallacy. Why? Because the line, the middle term, is not one and the self-same, but vari-riable. The terms, then, must not be variable, but one and the same. If either of them have a double meaning, it is no argument, but fallacy, *i. e.*, deception. Thus we arrive at the definition of fallacy. It is an apparent argument, which concludes contrary to truth. It must appear to be what it is not, or it would not deceive. We have also ascertained the cause of all fallacies in the process of argumentation, viz., the creation of a fourth *term*. Archbishop Whately divides fallacies into two classes—logical and non-logical. By logical fallacies he means those in which the fault lies in the reasoning process itself. By the non-logical, where the reasoning is correct in itself, but, from assuming some false position to start from, lands in error. The former class he subdivides variously; but I think they are all reducible to the one formula above stated, viz., the creation of a fourth term. A is equal to B, and C is equal to D. This gives no conclusion. My umbrella is as long as a stick; your flagstaff is as long as a stick; can you draw any conclusion? Why not? Because *a stick* is not a fixed quantity as thus stated. Fix the quantity—say the self-same stick—and the fallacy is removed. From the carpenter's process we see that an act of reasoning requires a measure—one common measure of two quantities ; and this is called the *middle term*. The clastic tape is not one length, but two or more. In like manner, if either of the other two terms, called the *major* and the *minor*, have a double meaning, there are four terms, and no argument. Take for example, the old sophism :

A church is a building of stone.

A company of Christians (associated for worship) is a church.

Therefore a company of Christians is a building of stone.

Here the word church has two meanings, and thus there are really four terms, though apparently but three. Logic has rules for detecting the various methods by which the fourth term is created, but we cannot go into detail.

Non-logical fallacies are those where the deception lies not in the reasoning process itself, but in the assumption of some false principle at the start. The thing assumed must lie covered up so as not to be apparent, or it will not deceive, and its detection requires close inspection of the premises. Herod reasoned thus when he inferred his obligation to kill John. He assumed as true what is false, viz., that an oath to do a wrong thing is binding.   The suicide reasons thus, when, from the principle that what is a man's own he may dispose of as he pleases, he concludes to destroy his own life.   The false assumption is that his life is his own, in the same sense that his money or his goods are his own.

It may be necessary only to add, that sometimes two fallacies, and of different classes, may meet in the same argument.   These we shall not illustrate until we find them in our progress.

The three angles of a triangle are equal to two right angles.   This proposition may be true, it may be false ; true, if you mean *jointly ;* false, if you mean *severally.*   These three boys, Joe, John, and James, are equal in height to Goliath of Gath : this is true, if they are taken *collectively ;* false, if *severally.*   So easy is it to divide a term into two, and thereby to create a fourth term in the syllogism, and of course, a fallacy.

7

CHAPTER XIV.

FALLACY—STATES INDEPENDENT.

Independent is a relative term ; it has reference to some other person, being, or thing, and suggests a negative idea. To depend is to hang from and upon. The apple upon the tree—it is pendent, *i. e.*, hanging from the branch, and is dependent for its position, absolute and relative, upon the tree. Now break the stem, it falls to the earth, and is not longer dependent for its position, but is independent on the tree. The child is dependent on its mother for food and protection, for instruction and education. He changes relations ; he is now a man ; he no longer hangs on his mother's bosom ; he is independent, *quoad hanc ;* but not absolutely ; for he stands related variously to other human beings. He depends upon society around him for enjoyment, for business and its results ; he depends on government for protection to life and liberty. A colony is a social infant, and, by necessity, is dependent in this stage of its being upon the mother country for support and protection. Even so late as 1754, Franklin speaks of England as "home"—"the government at *home.*" But this social infant, like the apple and the child, cannot remain always in the pendent condition ; relations must change in the onward flux of human affairs. The umbilical cord is cut, the infant has become a man, the colony a nation ; it is no longer pendent, or dependent as to the parent country, but is *independent.* It is a nation in fact, and if other nations admit the fact, it is a nation in form—one of the great family, dependent on self and mother earth alone.

But now, is this our history ? Was our nation *a* colony ? *One* colony ? Did Pennsylvania separately ever cut herself loose from the mother country ?—did Virginia ?—did South Carolina ? Then there are three independent nations ! The absurdity of this has been exposed in Chap. VI. Now we must glance at the fallacy based on, rather dependent on the historical absurdity.

The term is necessarily *relative.* To be independent has reference to other things—independent on what ? The Tartar dynasty ? The Sublime Porte ? The autocrat of all the Russias ? All this is true concerning the States severally, but was just as true before the Immortal Declaration as after it ; so the question reverts—independent on what ? The only true response is—on Britain. This is the one and only true meaning. But another construction has been foisted in upon this noble term. It means, say some, non-dependence on one another—each colony declared itself independent on every other. This fallacy is older than our Constitution ; for we find it in the Convention. (See Mad. Pap. p. 906.)

" Mr. Martin, Md., said, he considered that the separation from Great Britain placed the thirteen States in a state of nature toward each other ; that they would have remained in that state till this time, but for the confederation ; that they entered into the confederation on the footing of equality ; that they met now to amend it, on the same footing, and that he could never accede to a plan that would introduce an inequality, and lay ten States at the mercy of Virginia, Massachusetts, and Pennsylvania."

" Mr. Wilson, Penn., could not admit the doctrine that when the colonies became independent of Great Britain, they became independent also of each other. He read the Declaration of Independence, observing thereon, that the *United Colonies* were declared to be free and independent States ; and inferring that they were independent, not *individually*, but *unitedly*, and that they were confederated, as they were independent States."

"Colonel Hamilton assented to the doctrine of Mr. Wilson. He denied the doctrine that the States were thrown into a state of nature. He was not yet prepared to admit the doctrine that the confederacy could be dissolved by partial infractions of it."

"I hold it for a fundamental point, that an individual independence of the States is utterly irreconcilable with the idea of an aggregate sovereignty." (Mad. Papers, p. 631.)

Here we have the political heresy and its refutation. The Union, as we have seen, Chap. VI., was formed in 1774. Now we have to expose the logical heresy. The word is used in two senses—it means *independence* on Great Britain, in the first and true use ; but independence on the sister colonies, and all the world of nations, in the second and false sense. Let us syllogize it, thus :

An independent State may do as she pleases.
But South Carolina is an independent State.
Therefore, South Carolina may do as she pleases.

Here we have States' rights, States' sovereignty and secession, all demonstrated. But here we have the precise logical formula, which demonstrates a

body of pious Christians to be a building of stone !
How so ? Why, the middle term, *independent State*,
is used in one sense in the major premise, and in a
quite different sense in the minor ; hence we have
four terms, and, of course, no argument, but a miserable and bloody fallacy.

CHAPTER XV.

"But can you"—I was often asked before I left Virginia—"can you coerce a sovereign State?" Ask Mr. Edmund Randolph, certainly one of the safest and most profound sons of "the mother of States and of statesmen." What does he say in the Madison Papers, p. 732 : "That the national legislature ought to be empowered * * * to call forth the force of the Union against any member of the Union failing to fulfil its duty under the articles thereof." This was too strong mustard for Mr. Madison, who thought "the use of force against a State would look more like a declaration of war, than an infliction of punishment" (Mad. Pap. 761) ; and suggested to accomplish the object in another way. "Mr. Pinckney, South Carolina, moved, 'that the National Legislature should have authority to negative all laws [of States] which they should judge to be improper.' He urged that such a universality of the power was indispensably necessary to render it effectual ; that the States must be kept in due subordination to the nation ; that if the States were left to act of themselves, it would be impossible to defend the national prerogatives, however extensive they might be, on paper ; that the acts of Congress had been defeated by this means ; nor had foreign treaties escaped repeated violations ; that the universal negative was, in fact, the corner stone of an efficient National Government ; that under the British Government, the negative of the crown had been found beneficial, and the *States* are more one nation now than the *Colonies* were then." Pretty strong doctrine this for an illustrious predecessor of John C. Calhoun. But how did Virginia speak on this point ?   " Mr. Madison seconded the motion. He could not but regard an indefinite power to negative legislative acts of the States as absolutely necessary to a perfect system." (See Mad. Pap. p. 821-2.)

So far, however, as these quotations are arguments, they go only against the new generation of States' rights men. They are not my answer to the question, " Can you coerce a sovereign State ?" My answer ever was and is, *there never was a sovereign State.* The doctrine of sovereignty we have seen in Chap. IV. Our business now is to expose the fallacy of the question. We saw that sovereignty is an absolute unit only in the hand of

God ; that in human hands the distribution of ruling power is a necessity ; consequently, that the
lower functions are apportioned out to subordinate
officers, and only the higher reserved to the King,
President, Governor, Legislature, &c. So, in our
Providence-invented system, in the States is deposited, by the people, to whom God gave the whole, a
large and important part of the sovereignty, to be
by them exercised for their particular and special
benefit. These lower functions regard all the local
interests of the people near home and within the
sphere limited and bounded by the National Constitution. The General Government includes all
the higher functions of sovereignty which have been
delegated to it by the people of the whole nation, to
be exercised for the good of the whole. It is the
grand depository of the supreme functions ; the pon-
derous flywheel which regulates the movements of
the whole system of machinery ; the central sun,
whose attractive force preserves the unity of all the
surrounding planets, whilst its light guides them in
the paths they pursue.

You perceive, therefore, at a glance, that the
States are sovereign in a limited sense. All the attributes and functions of sovereignty not granted to
the General Government, remain still in the people,
except what they have severally vested in the State

Governments. So that we may truly say, *the States are sovereign ;* and we may as truly say, *the States are not sovereign.* Both propositions are true, but each in its own peculiar sense. They are sovereign within their own proper sphere ; they are not sovereign outside of their own sphere. I am supreme and sovereign in my own house ; in your house, I am not. Here then we have two different things expressed by one phrase—*a sovereign State.* In one, it means supreme power, or sovereignty, properly so called ; in the other, a limited portion of sovereign powers. To illustrate its operation, something like the following seems to have been an immensely practical argument about 1782 and 1832 :

A sovereign State cannot be coerced to pay taxes to another power.

But South Carolina is a sovereign State.

Therefore, South Carolina cannot be coerced to pay taxes to another power—the United States Government.

Under this reasoning, the cause of the country had wellnigh failed for want of revenue. But now here is the same error in logic. The first proposition is true, using the phrase, sovereign State, in the high and proper meaning. For obviously, if she is under bonds and force, she is not truly sovereign, but subordinate.   The second proposition is also true, but in another sense—a partial sovereignty only has she.   Here then, as before, the *middle term—sovereign State*—is divided into two, so we have four terms and no argument, but a miserable and bloody fallacy.

It may be useful to notice the composition of these two fallacies by the combination of the terms, sovereign and independent States ; or by calling the States *independent sovereignties.*   This constitutes a fallacy of the second class.

CHAPTER XVI.

FALLACY—GRATUITOUS ASSUMPTION: THE STATES ARE INDEPENDENT SOVEREIGNTIES.

THIS runs through all the argumentations of the States' rights men, the nullifiers, the secessionists. Rather it is the basis of their operations ; down it comes to even Mr. Jefferson Davis ! The second paragraph of his first inaugural contains it—" the sovereign States "—" they, as sovereign States, were final judges " when they should withdraw. " Thus the sovereign States here represented." And in his second message, April 29, 1861, he assumes it as the basis of his argument ; in the progress of which, nevertheless, he quotes the very article of the Confederation (Art. II.) which affirms the limitation of the powers of the States and affirms their dependence on one another. True he misquotes the Article, thus : " In order to guard against any misconstruction of their compact, the several States made an explicit declaration in a distinct article, that each State retains its sovereignty, freedom and independence, and every power of jurisdiction and right which

is not, by this said Confederation, expressly delegated to the United States in Congress assembled under this contract of alliance." (See Rebellion Record, Doc., p. 167.) Such is Mr. Davis's reading ;
we turn to the record :

" Art. II. Each State retains its sovereignty,
freedom and independence, and every power, jurisdiction and right, which is not by this Confederation expressly delegated to the United States in
Congress assembled."

The reader will observe the difference, whilst we
note the purpose for which he adduces the Article,
viz., to prove the absolute independence and sovereignty of the States ; whereas it expressly asserts,
that parts and portions of both are already delegated
to the United States in Congress assembled. Yet
the whole force of his argument is based on the assumed, but disproved fact, of their absolute sovereignty and independence. These gentlemen all affirm the unqualified and unlimited right of each
State to judge and determine, by itself alone, without let or hindrance, whether it will secede from the
Union or not, and when it will secede. That is,
they claim for each the highest sovereignty and
most absolute independence, and they prove the
soundness of their claim by citing Article II., which
in most express terms asserts the contrary !

In Chaps. XIV. and XV. we have disproved this doctrine and exposed the fallacies which, very possibly, have led many unconsciously to entertain these two dangerous falsehoods. Here we wish only to show up the two deceptions as combined in the one gratuitous assumption of independent State sovereignty. This *assumed*, the reasoning which establishes the right of secession is sound.

If the States are sovereign and independent nations, then of course it follows, that they have a right to declare war, establish peace, form alliances, make treaties, &c. &c. But even then, it does not follow that they have a right to annul treaties, &c., at pleasure. But even sound reasoning, from a false premise, leads to the discovery and establishment of truth, never.

If, however, under the Articles of Confederation, the States retained but a limited sovereignty, protected by their league of friendship, and where the whole instrument purports to be a Confederation, as we have seen in Chap. IX., how much less ground is there for an independent State sovereignty, under the Constitution, which ignores most particularly, as we have seen in Chap. XII., both the name and the thing ?

"This right to secede," says General Jackson, "is deduced from the nature of the Constitution,

which they [the nullifiers] say, is a compact between sovereign States who have preserved their
whole sovereignty, and therefore are subject to no
superior ; that because they made the compact,
they can break it, when in their opinion it has been
departed from by the other States. Fallacious as
this course of reasoning is, it enlists State pride,"
&c. (See Statesman's Manual, p. 800.)

"The Constitution of the United States, then,
forms a government, not a league, and whether it
be formed by compact between the States, or in
any other manner, its character is the same. It is
a government in which all the people are represented, which operates directly on the people individually, and not upon the States—they [the peo-
ple] retained all the power they did not grant.
But each State, having expressly parted with so
many powers as to constitute,. jointly with the
other States, a single nation, cannot from that period possess any right to secede, because such secession does not break a league, but destroys the
unity of a nation, and any injury to that unity is
not only a breach which would result from the
contravention of a compact, but it is an offence
against the whole Union. To say that any State
may secede from the Union, is to say, that the
United States are not a nation, because it would

be a solecism to contend that any part of a nation might dissolve its connection with the other parts, to their injury or ruin, without committing any offence. Secession, like any other revolutionary act, may be morally justified by the extremity of oppression ; but to call it a constitutional right, is confounding the meaning of terms, and can only be done through gross error, or to deceive those who are willing to assert a right, but would pause before they made a revolution, or incur the penalties consequent on a failure.

"Because the Union was formed by compact, it is said, the parties to that compact may, when they feel themselves aggrieved, depart from it ; but it is precisely because it is a compact, that they cannot. A compact is an agreement or binding obligation, &c., &c."

On p. 802 General Jackson proceeds : "The States severally have not retained their entire sovereignty. It has been shown that, in becoming parts of a nation, not members of a league, they surrendered many of their essential parts of sovereignty. The right to make treaties, declare war, levy taxes, exercise exclusive judicial and legislative powers, were all of them functions of sovereign power. [He might have added naturalization of foreigners, which belonged to the States under the

Articles, but is given by the Constitution to the United States.] The States, then, for all those important purposes, were no longer sovereign. The allegiance of their citizens was transferred, in the first instance, to the Government of the United States; they became American citizens, and owed obedience to the Constitution of the United States, and to laws made in conformity with the powers vested in Congress." On p. 806, having pointed out the unparalleled prosperity and happiness of the country, especially of the people of South Carolina, to whom the proclamation is addressed, he proceeds: "And for what, mistaken men! for what do you throw away these inestimable blessings—for what would you exchange your share in the advantages and honor of the Union? For the dream of a separate independence—a dream interrupted by bloody conflicts with your neighbors, and a vile dependence on foreign power. If your leaders could succeed in establishing a separation, what would be your situation? Are you united at home—are you free from the apprehension of civil discord with all its fearful consequences? Do our neighboring republics, every day suffering some new revolution or contending with some new insurrection—do they excite your envy? But the dictates of a high duty oblige me solemnly to announce that you cannot succeed. The laws of the United States must be executed. I have no discretionary power on the subject—my duty is emphatically pronounced in the Constitution. Those who told you that you might peaceably prevent their execution, deceived you—they could. not have been deceived themselves. They know that a forcible opposition could alone prevent the execution of the laws, and they know that such opposition must be repelled. Their object is disunion ; but be not deceived by names : disunion by armed force, is *treason.* Are you really ready to incur its guilt ? " Oh ! *si sic omnes.* If a Jackson had been in the Presidential chair, we should not now be in the midst of a bloody rebellion.

CHAPTER XVII.

POLITICO-ECCLESIASTICO DISCUSSION — FALLACIES EXPOSED.

DOCTOR SPRING'S RESOLUTIONS IN THE GENERAL ASSEMBLY OF THE PRESBYTERIAN CHURCH—HISTORY AND REMARKS.

THESE five following chapters have a peculiar type, indicated, obscurely indeed, by the above caption. They involve discussions of the great matters before the nation—fealty, loyalty, Christian duty in these times. They are not religious, properly speaking, nor ecclesiastical ; and, though they have phrases adapted especially to interest Presbyterians, yet the essence of the whole will prove, I doubt not, as interesting as any of the preceding ; because the arguments examined are common, and regard the duties of all sects—and of no sect. The XVIIIth and XXIst have no relation to anything peculiar to any denomination.

On the morning of the 18th of May " Dr. Spring offered a resolution, that a Special Committee be appointed to inquire into the expediency of this

Assembly making some expression of their devotion to the Union of these States and their loyalty to the Government ; and if, in their judgment, it is expedient so to do, they report what that expression shall be." (See Min. Gen. Assem., p. 303.)

"On motion of Mr. Hoyte, this resolution was laid on the table, by a vote 123 to 102."

Remark : 1. On a motion of simple inquiry, a refusal seldom occurs in any body where free discussion is allowed. Nothing but some evident, glaring impropriety ever occasions a refusal of a committee to inquire. But such impropriety, the vote here, and the subsequent action of the body, prove had no existence.

2. A motion to lay on the table a resolution before discussion, and especially if the mover is a respectable man, not given to be troublesome, is, to say the least, *discourteous*. It contains a severe rebuke. But to take *snap judgment*, if you will pardon the expression, on a man so aged, so venerable, so dignified, gentlemanly, and courteous, and withal so universally admired and beloved throughout the churches, seems to me altogether outside of the amenities of Christian intercourse.

3. This impropriety — this want of delicate Christian sensibility — is greatly enhanced by the source of the motion to lay on the table. A Ten-

nesseean, at least, ought to have shrunk from it. Surely it ought to have been left for some Northerner—neighbor to Dr. Spring.

"A call for the 'yeas and nays,' to be recorded, was made by Mr. Robertson, after the members had begun to vote by rising, which the Moderator declared to be out of order." This decision, absurd as it is, was not appealed from. It is the usual course, when it is obvious that there is a close vote and that it is exceedingly difficult to count so large a number accurately, to resort to the yeas and nays as the only way to insure certainty, and such is the rule parliamentary; and this may be done even after the vote is taken.

"After the result had been announced, Mr. H. K. Clarke moved to take this resolution up from the table, and on this motion called for the yeas and nays."

This occasioned discussions about points of order—for the rule forbids discussion of the motion to take off the table—until Wednesday morning, May 22, when, to cut off such discussion, "Dr. Spring offered a paper with resolutions respecting the appointment of religious solemnities for the 4th of July next, and the duty of ministers and churches in relation to the condition of the country; which, on motion of Dr. Hodge, was made the

first order of the day for Friday morning next."
(Min., p. 308.)

For a whole week, off and on, these resolutions
were discussed with great zeal and ability. Various amendments, substitutes, &c., were offered, and
one strenuous effort was put forth to lay the whole
subject on the table, which motion, made by Dr.
Hodge, was decided by ayes 87, and noes 153.
The final vote was taken on Wednesday evening,
May 29—ayes 156, noes 66.

It is unfortunate that Dr. Spring's resolutions
were not put on the record until after all discussion, amendments, &c., were ended ; so that the
reader cannot easily learn what the originals were.
But as finally adopted, they stand thus :

" Gratefully acknowledging the distinguished
bounty and care of Almighty God toward this
favored land, and also recognizing our obligations
to submit to every ordinance of man for the Lord's
sake, this General Assembly adopt the following
resolutions :

" *Resolved*, 1. That in view of the present
agitated and unhappy state of this country, the
1st day of July next [Dr. Spring had it the 4th,
the day on which Congress was to meet] be hereby
set apart as a day of prayer throughout our land ;
and that on this day ministers and people are called

on humbly to confess and bewail our national sins; to offer our thanks to the Father of lights for His abundant and undeserved goodness toward us as a nation ; to seek His guidance and blessing upon our rulers and their counsels, as well as on the Congress of the United States about to assemble; and to implore Him, in the name of Jesus Christ, the great High Priest of the Christian profession, to turn away his anger from us, and speedily restore to us the blessings of an honorable peace.

"*Resolved*, 2. That this General Assembly, in the spirit of that Christian patriotism which the Scriptures enjoin, and which has always characterized this Church, do hereby acknowledge and declare our obligations to promote and perpetuate, so far as in us lies, the integrity of these United States, and to strengthen, uphold, and encourage the Federal Government in the exercise of all its functions under our noble Constitution ; and to this Constitution, in all its provisions, requirements, and principles, we profess our unabated loyalty.

" And to avoid all misconception, the Assembly declare that by the terms 'Federal Government,' as here used, is not meant any particular administration, or the particular opinions of any particular party, but that central administration which, being at any time appointed and inaugurated according to the forms prescribed in the Constitution of the United States, is the visible representative of our national existence." (Min., 331.)

I have placed the whole matter adopted by the Assembly before the reader, although the first paragraph of the second resolution alone will come under the following discussion. The second paragraph was not in Dr. Spring's resolution, but was appended by the Assembly. It may be proper to say that the doctor was taken ill, and left at an early part of the discussions, in which he can scarcely be said to have participated.

Before proceeding to the main object of this chapter, viz., the exposition of the fallacy which pervades the arguments against the resolution, a few general remarks seem proper. A majority, I hope, of my readers know nothing of the ecclesiastical relations of this matter, and are therefore the better qualified to judge the resolution simply on its merits. What does it teach ?

1. Here is a simple acknowledgment and declaration of a fact. "This General Assembly do acknowledge and declare." There is not the semblance of an authoritative dictum of a legislative or judicial body : no command, no order, no decree, no injunction upon any human being or class of beings, ordering them to do or not to do anything

whatsoever. It is a simple declaration of a *fact.*   •

2. This fact is, that *obligations* lie, not upon you, or Napoleon III, or Pio Nino, or the members of the church at Smyrna, or New Orleans, or the church of Nashville ; nothing at all of all this,—but *on us—our obligations. We,* the General Assembly, do declare the fact—obligations lie *on us.* Had this body, *i. e.,* a majority, a right to declare this fact ? Assuredly, if it was true, they had ; if it was not true, they had not. But suppose some thought it was not true ; they felt no such obligation : must they, are they bound to assert a falsehood ? No ; they are bound to say *no,* to tell the truth, and say they feel no obligations to

3. Promote and perpetuate the integrity of these United States. This is the first obligation declared and acknowledged. On whom does it lie ? On us—our obligation. To promote and perpetuate is *not enjoined*—is not *commanded.* No obligation is created by this act, nor attempted or professed to be created. But simply the preëxistent, the always existent obligation, is acknowledged and declared—to perpetuate the Union.

4. But even this is not conceived or expressed to be absolute. An unlimited obligation to promote and perpetuate the Union is not declared to

8

be on us; but only "so far as in us lies." If, then,
Mr. Hoyte or Dr. Backus are so situated that they
can do nothing at all toward promoting and per-
petuating the integrity of the United States, there
is not here even a declaration of obligation lying
upon them; absolutely nothing.

5. And this qualification, "so far as in us lies,"
extends to every one of the things in reference to
which the Assembly acknowledges "our obligations."

6. Here is a profession of faith and attachment
unabated to our Constitution. There is no command, order, or decree laid upon any human being;
but a simple declaration of a fact—"our unabated
loyalty." If, then, any man does not *feel* it, let
him not say it. We, the Assembly lay no hand on
him: no such idea is anywhere found in any part
of any of the Spring resolutions. And yet,

7. In the face of these facts, in the very teeth
of this resolution, it was affirmed in the discussion to be an usurpation of power, a decree of
excision, leading to schism in the church; and this,
although all the church knew that the decree of
schism had gone forth from Columbia, the ruling
centre of the South. The Presbytery of Charleston
had appointed commissioners to this very Assembly;
but the guns against Sumter woke up the lion,

who, by the by, was not asleep ; a *pro re nata* meeting of Presbytery was called, the commissions were revoked, and the steps inaugurated for secession from the Presbyterian Church in these United States. Others followed suit. The Presbytery of Lexington appointed their commissioners before I left it. South Carolina moved, and the commissioners never attended—they were dragged out. This resolution, it was affirmed, made new terms of communion—subverted the Constitution, and forced men to pray and work for the Union, when it was sure to lead to their execution. In my brief span of experience I certainly never saw such an extended discussion, and so ably and zealously conducted, entirely aside from and outside of the paper from which it started. This was owing to the warmth of the opponents and their excited imaginations. They having gone on to this ground, their opponents followed them in the wild chase. But the grand mistake of all remains to be pointed out, and must be the subject of a distinct chapter.

CHAPTER XVIII.

THIS dialogue between Captain Smith and his pastor, Rev. Mr. Brown, is thrown in here because the principle vindicated by Mr. Brown comes in necessarily in the discussions of the succeeding chapters.

Captain Smith.—Good morning, Mr. Brown! I hope I see you well after the hard service of Sunday.

Pastor Brown.—Thanks to our good Master, I am nothing the worse of the labors of the Sabbath; but I don't quite like the expression *hard*, which you apply to the services of the holy day. I often think of the remark of old Father Scrimgeour, a devoted and godly Scotch preacher of New York State, who used to say, "Preaching has been often the worse of me, but I have never been the worse of preaching."

Capt. S.—Very true; but you seemed yesterday

to exert yourself so vigorously, that I supposed you must feel uneasy and Mondayish this morning. You did pour it upon them with all your might. By the way, Mr. Brown, did you know you gave a little offence to some of your hearers, by your remarks about whiskey, bribery, and the tricks and schemes of the demagogues, about these election times?

Mr. B.—Sorry for that; I certainly didn't wish to wound the feelings of any sinner improperly, and God forbid that I should sin against the generation of the just. Who is it that I have offended?

Capt. S.—Old Tom Harris thinks you came a little too close on him in your remarks about whiskey and bacon; and, indeed, considering he's so poor, and has unfortunately got such a habit of drinking, he seems as if he couldn't help it; and I pitied the poor dog, and thought, at the time, that perhaps it would be better not to bring politics into the pulpit at all. I've long thought there was truth in the proverb, " Religion has nothing to do with politics ; " and, to be candid, you came so close sometimes, that I began to wince myself; for, you know, I'm a little of a politician, too.

Mr. B.—Well, it's true I do cut pretty close sometimes; but then, you see, it seems to come right in my way. How could I expound the language of my text, and show the character of the good man, "who walketh righteously, and speaketh uprightly; he that despiseth the gain of oppressions, that shaketh his hands from holding of bribes,"—without saying something which must make men wince who act differently? I vowed at my ordination to "preach the word," whether men will hear or whether they will forbear. There's another proverb worthy of recollection: "If the shoe fits you, put it on." My sworn duty is to present to my hearers the plain meaning of the word, leaving it to conscience and to the Holy Spirit to bring it home to the individuals to whom it is adapted.

Capt. S.—Ay, but these election times, when we politicians are somewhat excited and on the sharp lookout, it appears as if it might be prudent (excuse my freedom) to bear off politics, at least till we get time to cool down.

Mr. B.—That is plausible, and I don't at all wonder that you feel so. But then, my dear sir, just look at the matter from my standpoint: "Reprove, rebuke, exhort, with all long suffering and doctrine." Now, does it seem common sense to reprove and rebuke evils that have no existence at the time and place? Should not the blister be laid where the inflammation is, and at the time? Besides, Captain, your proverb, *Religion has nothing to do with politics*, has, perhaps, led you into a mistake in your reasoning. I, on the contrary, affirm that religion is the very foundation of politics.

Capt. S.—Oh! that'll never do. We'll differ entirely; here is a direct contradiction. If you take this ground, you'll be everlastingly preaching against the Democrats, or the Whigs, or the Republicans, the secession rebels or the loyal Unionists; and we'll get no gospel at all.

Mr. B.—Not quite so fast, Captain. There is another scripture which I try to keep in mind: "Rightly dividing the word of truth, giving to every man his portion of meat in due season." Besides, Captain, we don't differ much, after all. Your proverb and mine are not contradictory, as you suppose, but both are true, when you come to understand the meaning of the terms; and if you will bear with me, I will endeavor to explain wherein you are deceived by the vague, equivocal, double meaning of a word. The term *politics,* in your proverb, means partyism, political management, tricks of faction, duplicity, deception, wirepulling, frauds upon the purity of elections, whiskey and other bribery, pipelaying, and all the thousand devices that go to make up the character of the demagogue. So, *he's a great politician* means that the man is up to all these—he's an adept in them. Now, in this sense, I perfectly agree with you, religion has nothing to do with politics. Surely there is no religion in all these. So there we are agreed.

But there is another sense in which the word *politics* is used. It includes great knowledge of political affairs—the principles of government—the very nature of man in regard to society, to law, to justice, to social order, to national and international affairs. Thus, we say, Washington, Jefferson, the Adamses, Madison, Jay, Franklin, Morris, &c., were profound politicians. They had studied with great success the principles of political science and economy. I like their politics—*i. e.*, their sentiments, their doctrines in reference to political affairs. When, therefore, I say that religion is the foundation of politics, I don't differ from you in regard to things. The difference lies merely in the meaning of a term.

Capt. S.—Oh, very well. I'm glad to find we agree as to principle. To be sure, there is no sure foundation for civil government but the moral law. If we abandon the pure doctrines of the Bible, we can never build up a political fabric that will endure ; and I have always understood that our great politicians, judges, statesmen, have declared Christianity to be a part of the common law.

Mr. B.—But, Captain, I noticed you said *principle*—I agree with you in *principle*. If so, we cannot greatly differ in practice. Yet, allow me to point out the fallacy which had almost made us to differ. It lies in the double meaning of the word *politics*. In Chapter XIII we have seen that logical fallacies are generated by the creation of a fourth term ; and here we have it. You compare religion with politics, in one sense, and perceive that they differ, and hence you infer that ministers ought to abstain from preaching politics, and find fault with me because I preach politics, which I do in quite the other sense. I advocate no party principles or party chicanery ; but simply expound the doctrines of the moral law, and apply them in rebuking and reproving the misdeeds of political partisans and all others.

Here we have, then, the devil's *double entendre*, by the adroit use of which he has succeeded to a large degree in paralyzing the pulpit and destroying its power for good over one large portion of its appropriate field. Under this fallacy, politicians have become a privileged class. They occupy a sphere within which "the reproofs of instruction, which are the way of life," must not. presume to enter. With regard to lying, swearing, treating, drunkenness, bribery, Sabbath electioneering, &c., &c., connected with political management, this fallacy cries, "Hands off, preachers ! This ground

8*

is appropriated to his Satanic Majesty. He has turned politician, and religion has nothing to do with politics ; ergo, shut up, and 'let us alone ; ' art thou come to torment us before the time ? "

And now, my dear Captain, I must close ; and I leave for your serious consideration the following question, viz. : When the devil claims his own and carries off the *politician*, where will the *man* be found ?

CHAPTER XIX.

THIS is the main position of the opponents; and, as it involves the subject of moral obligation to government, its discussion here will, I hope, aid in settling the true doctrine, by exposing the fallacy by which gigantic efforts were put forth for its overthrow.

It is agreed, on all hands, that Church and State have each their own proper sphere within which to act; whilst it is sometimes difficult to run the division line with precision between them. Both in the Assembly of 1861 and 1862 the Confession of the Presbyterian Church, chap. 31, sec. 4, was cited in their favor by the protestants: "Synods and councils are to handle and conclude nothing but that which is ecclesiastical; and are not to intermeddle in civil affairs which concern the commonwealth, unless by way of humble petition in cases extraordinary; or by way of advice for

the satisfaction of conscience, if they be thereunto
required by the civil magistrate." Hence, it was
triumphantly concluded, this resolution is condemned; and this by men of sound, logical minds!
It was plainly evident, nevertheless, that they perceived not at all their perfectly gratuitous assumption, that the *resolution* aimed to settle a political
question, and was therefore *intermeddling*, in the
sense of the Confession. But now, this was the
very point in dispute. To declare *our obligations*
to obey magistrates, to be loyal, "so far as in us
lies," to support our Government—is this a political
question? Or is it of the very highest morality?
None of these brethren ever thought love of country, love to civil officers, obedience to all their lawful commands, belonged to the domain prohibited
to the church; for they all know that a large part
of the church's duty is to inculcate these virtues,
and also to censure for their neglect. When Peter
(1st Ep., chap. ii, 13, 14) commanded, "Submit
yourselves to every ordinance of man, for the Lord's
sake; whether it be to the king, as supreme; or
unto governors, as unto them that are sent by him
for the punishment of evil doers and for the praise
of them that do well,"—did he intermeddle with
civil affairs? What is intermeddling? It is, lit-
erally and truly, coming in between another person

or party and his proper duty or business, so as to hinder or obstruct its performance. Or, as the Assembly's able and conclusive answer to the protest puts it, did Christ intermeddle when he said, "Render to Cæsar the things that are Cæsar's"?

Besides, this citation from the Confession bears against the protestants in another way: Synods are not to intermeddle, "unless by way of humble petition in cases extraordinary." I suppose ours is a case extraordinary; and yet the Assembly did not go the length even of humble petition to the civil powers. Some brethren, indeed, of the opposition, did telegraph to Attorney-General Bates, to get his counsel and aid in support of their cause; but the Assembly kept within their own proper sphere, and did not even give a side glance to the peculiar province of the civil magistrate. Let the opponents of the *resolution* prove that it intermeddles in civil affairs, and their business is concluded; but a sweeping *petitio principii* is not a logical finality.

It is sometimes important in controversy (and there are people who think it *very* important) to ascertain what is the precise point in dispute. In the present case, the Spring *resolution* was not the point. The doctrine it contains was, with very nearly perfect unanimity, considered true and proper—abstractly sound and good—and all men approved it. Dr.

Hodge, the author of the protest, and indisputably the ablest debater in the opposition, uses very strong language : " We make this protest, not because we do not acknowledge loyalty to our country to be a moral and religious duty, according to the word of God, which requires us to be subject to the powers that be ; nor because we deny the right of the Assembly to enjoin that and all other like duties on the ministers and churches under its care ; but because we deny the right of the General Assembly to decide the political question, to what government the allegiance of Presbyterians, as citizens, is due, and its right to make that decision a condition of membership in our church." (See Min., p. 339.)   This last, as to a condition of membership, we have seen is utterly a mistake : nothing of the kind is contained in the resolution, and, of course, nothing of the kind is inferable from it.   But here is a full acknowledgment of the right and authority of a church court to teach and enforce all duties of loyalty as moral and religious.   Again he says (Princeton Review, 1861, p. 559) : " We believe the course of the South, in its attempt to break up our glorious Union, is unreasonable, ungrateful, and wicked.   We believe that the war in which the Government is now engaged is entirely righteous, necessary for the preservation of our existence as a nation, and for the security of the rights, liberty, and well being, not only of this generation, but of generations yet unborn. We believe that it is the duty of every man in these United States to do all that in him lies 'to strengthen, sustain, and encourage the Federal Government in the conflict in which it is now engaged.'" This is extremely satisfactory. What, then, is wrong? What is the point in controversy? If we succeed in answering this question, we shall probably succeed in exposing the fallacy. The first step, according to old Walton, toward cooking a sturgeon, is to catch him. Where is he? Just here: "The General Assembly has no right to decide the political question, to what Government the allegiance of Presbyterians, as citizens, is due."

In like manner, the paper adopted by the Synod of Kentucky, which was drawn up by Dr. R. J. Breckinridge, the strongest and most heroic defender of the right on these questions, asserts "the subject matter of the action of the Assembly, in the premises, being *purely political,* was incompetent to a spiritual court. Undoubtedly it was *incompetent* to the Assembly, as a spiritual court, to require or to advise acts of disobedience to *actual governments* by those under the power of those governments."

In like manner, the Presbytery of Louisville says : "The assumption of power to determine questions of political allegiance is directly contrary to the teachings of Christ and his apostles, who uniformly enjoin obedience to Cæsar as a Christian duty, but abstain from determining as between the claims of rival Cæsars to the allegiance of Christians."

Two points, undoubtedly, are taken by these gentlemen : 1st. That the question involved in the Spring resolutions is purely political, as contradistinguished from moral and religious ; viz., to which of *two governments* Presbyterians owe allegiance.

2d. That the church has no right and power to decide this question.

Their argument, logically stated, is thus :

The decision of a question purely political, is not within the church's power.

But the Spring resolutions are a decision of a question purely political :

Therefore, the Spring resolutions are not within the church's power.

We concede the major—we admit that purely political questions lie without the sphere of church authority. The battle field, therefore, is the minor premise, and, as it is an affirmative proposition, the

onus probandi lies upon those who claim the conclusion ; and we shall certainly not yield it to them
until they may and shall have proved that this is a
purely political matter. This has been attempted,
especially in their protest and its defence in the
Princeton Review. And the first response we
make is an *ad hominem* to that distintinguished
and able advocate. In the number for July, 1862,
p. 515, he says : "We remarked on the floor of the
last Assembly, that we would cheerfully vote for
Dr. Spring's resolutions, if introduced into the
Synod of New Jersey, although constrained to vote
against them as the decisions of the Assembly.
Those resolutions declare it to be the duty of our
Southern brethren to maintain the integrity of the
Union, and to sustain the General Government."
And is it not the duty of our Jersey brethren to
sustain the General Govenrment ? Are there no disciples of Calhoun in that Synod ? If the Spring
resolutions contain a political question in the Assembly, why not in the Synod ? Is there no branch
of the Knights of the Golden Circle in New Jersey ?
in Pennsylvania ? in Ohio ? in Indiana ? in Maryland ? Why not refuse to vote for the resolutions
in these localities, for the benefit of the band sworn
to assassinate Abraham Lincoln ?

2. Another special *ad hominem*. The Review

lays great stress on the representation in fact present in the Assembly. The protest says : " It was,
in our judgment, unfair to entertain and decide such
a momentous question, when the great majority of
our Southern Presbyterians were, from necessity,
unrepresented in this body." To this the Assembly responds : " We need only reply, that the roll
of this Assembly shows delegates from Virginia,
Kentucky, Missouri, Tennessee, Mississippi, Louisiana, and Texas. All might have been easily
represented." But the Princeton Review (1862,
p. 516) says : " The Assembly of 1861, representing the South as well as the North, did decide a
grave political question. The Assembly of 1862,
representing only the loyal States, decided no such
question, but simply enjoined a duty, which binds
all for whom the Assembly acted, no matter how
that political question may be decided." We leave
these two to face one another on the line of contradiction, with the remark, that in the Assembly of
1861, there were forty-one, or, omitting six in
foreign lands, thirty-five Presbyteries unrepresented ; and in that of 1862, sixty-seven, out of one
hundred and sixty-seven, or, omitting six in
foreign countries, sixty-one. Surely it is not intended to affirm the doctrine, that Presbyteries
not represented through their own delinquency
have ground of complaint in this fact ; or that the

action of the Assembly properly affects only those represented. Can they take advantage of their own wrong ?

3. The Review admits (1861, p. 542) the point in debate : "Under these circumstances the General Assembly was called upon to take sides. This had been an easy and obvious duty, if all Presbyterians represented in the Assembly, and whose organ it was, had been of one mind on the subject. But, alas ! this was not so." And why was it not so ? Was it the fault of the 156 ayes or of the 66 noes ? Yes, it is easy to decide when all are of one mind ; but if a minority dissent and steadfastly hold their position, must the majority succumb, and waive their duty, and their rights forego ? This is Calhounism—Davisism, of the most recent stamp. Mr. Jefferson Davis, in his message in April, 1861, says : "And so utterly have the principles of the Constitution been corrupted in the Northern mind, that in the inaugural address delivered by President Lincoln in March last, he asserts, as an axiom which he plainly deems to be undeniable, that the theory of the Constitution requires that in all cases the majority shall govern." (Reb. Rec., vol. i, Doc., p. 168.) Here is the aristocratic idea which the Constitution of the United States is bound to put down when, it guarantees to every State a re-

publican form of government. Now, are we to have aristocracy also in the church, and must minorities govern ? If South Carolina chooses to be in the Assembly, by her commissioners, then the majority may govern, unless South Carolina should happen to differ in opinion from the rest. Then and in that case the minority must govern. And our brethren must either admit this, or grant the right of secession in the church. Why were not the Southern Presbyteries in the last two Assemblies ? Because they did not choose to be where they could not control by majorities or minorities. Was it not notorious at Indianapolis and at Rochester, that the Southern Presbyteries were then preparing to secede ? Why, the Princeton Review substantially admits the fact. (See p. 556, 1861.) Must the Northern and Western Presbyteries wait until the Southern choose to come up ? Here is schism, and the right is claimed to secede at pleasure ; and, as was before said, they have exercised the reserved right. In view of these facts, it is worse than idle for our brethren to dirge out jeremiads prophetic over the divisions which the Spring resolutions will produce. Who was it that exercised the right of secession ? *When* was it ? Undeniably, *before* the Assembly of 1861 met, South Carolina seceded *de facto* from the Presbyterian Church.

4. Both the Kentucky Synod's paper and the Presbyterian Review assume that the Presbyterians in the South must either be absent from the Assembly, and not pray for the United States Government, or be tried for treason and hung. Poor, unfortunate men ! And this wicked General Assembly and that cruel and hard-hearted Father Spring shut them up to the dire alternative of schism or the gallows. These thoughts pervaded all the discussions. Oh ! this cruel resolution. Brethren ! spare your sympathy and tears. These Southern Presbyterians are either laughing at your simplicity, or pitying your stupidity.

For, first, it is notorious that they held the controlling power in their hands. I could name half a dozen of Presbyterian ministers who could have arrested the secession, if they had seen fit. Notoriously, the Presbyterian ministers of the South were the leading spirits of the rebellion. It could not have been started without them. That stupendous victory, won by ten thousand of the unconquerable chivalry, over Robert Anderson and his seventy-two half-starved soldiers, after thirty-six hours of heavy cannonading, could never have been achieved but for the encouraging shouts of Rev. James H. Thornwell, D.D., and Rev. Benjamin M. Palmer, D.D.

But, secondly, even in the Border States, the

Presbyterian ministers alone, if they had had a moiety of the heroic, martyr spirit of Robert J. Breckinridge, could have shut up the sluices of treason and turned the battle from the gates. All that was needed was to present a solid front, and the demon spirit would have cowered before them, and slunk back to his own den. Had my beloved brother Dr. White and his twelve Union elders stood firmly together, all the demons of pandemonium and Charleston too could not have driven them from Rockbridge county, and forced treason and rebellion on a people who had voted more than ten to one in favor of the Union candidates for the convention.

But, thirdly, it were better to die a martyr to religious liberty and the oaths they had taken to support the Constitution of the United States, than to be dragooned into treason, perjury, and rebellion. Posterity will know who are more respected and esteemed in history, Dr. Breckinridge or Dr. Palmer. The newspapers report that Breckinridge has been seized by the guerilla bands : be it so ; they cannot conquer him, and they dare not hang him. God is his shield and buckler. The assassin's dagger cannot reach those whom Divine power would protect. Kentucky and Tennessee have a pledge of their ultimate redemption in the unconquerable spirit of such heroic men.

One other point of weakness in the minor premise is the fact, admitted too by the very men whose argument it destroys, that war was begun on Fort Sumter at half past four o'clock on the morning of Friday, April 13th; that the first glorious victory of secession—first except by false syllogisms—had occurred, on the 15th, when the fort surrendered; that the victorious general, all hanging over with laurel, and a great army in his train, was on his march for Washington, with the avowed purpose of capturing that city. On the 10th of May, nineteen days before the adoption of the obnoxious resolutions, Major-General R. E. Lee was ordered by the rebel secretary to the command of the army in Virginia. In short, secession had, as its nature required, eventuated in rebellion and civil war. Now the gentlemen admit (see protest) that "loyalty to our country is a moral and religious duty,"—that treason and perjury are sins, and that it is the duty of the Assembly to bear witness against sins of all kinds. It is notoriously untrue, therefore, that the resolution is political. Its drift and purport, and design and end and object, is to rebuke the bloody spirit of war then waging, and the treason which generated that war. The minor premise is glaringly false, and the argument no argument at all; but a most bloody fallacy.

CHAPTER XX.

THE GRAND FALLACY—THE GRATUITOUS AND FALSE
ASSUMPTION THAT THE SOUTHERN REBELLION IS A
GOVERNMENT.

THE man who stands on the locomotive, lever in
hand, governs the engine. His management of it
is a government. The two balls, the levers, the
pins, joints, &c., which regulate the steam upon the
engine in the mint, at the factory, the grist mill, are
called a *governor*, and this regulating influence is a
government. The management of a gang of laborers on the turnpike, the ruling influence over a squad
of soldiers, of policemen, of children in a school, is a
government. The management of religious matters
in a church, and of civil matters in a state, is a *government*. Now this infinite variety of meanings
must be kept in view when we say the Southern
rebellion is not a government—it has not resulted
in a government. Virginia, South Carolina, Pennsylvania is not a government—is not a sovereign
power—is not a nation. We speak of the Government of the United States, and the Government of

Pennsylvania ; but by the former we mean very differently from the latter : this is not a power in the sense of the Bible, that is, a power supreme. In short, analogous distinctions exist here to those pointed out in Chap. IV., in regard to sovereignty. The phrase *United States Government* has a clear and well defined meaning the world over. All nations understand it as designating an independent, sovereign power, having all the rights, privileges, prerogatives of absolute supremacy ; there is no power above it ; it is amenable to none but God. None can dictate law to it or call it to account, but for violations of international law ; and that only by war. Now, in this highest sense, I deny the proposition that the Confederate States of America, so self-named,—the C. S. A.,—is a government, and that any State is a government. (See Chaps. VI. and VII.) The converse of this proposition is the fallacy of fallacies on this whole subject, and it pervades the entire argumentations of those who oppose the Spring resolutions : it is a *petitio principii*.

The protest (see Min. 1861, p. 339) states it thus : " We deny the right of the General Assembly to decide the political question, to what government the allegiance of Presbyterians, as citizens, is due," *i. e.*, two governments, viz., the United States on the one hand, and the State of South Carolina,

9

or the C. S. A., on the other.   Now the question is, to which of the two is that allegiance due ?

Again, same page, " The question is whether the allegiance of our citizens is primarily due to the State or to the Union." Here are *two governments* claiming allegiance—or, as Lord Coke defines allegiance, " the highest and greatest obligation of duty and obedience that can be." Allegiance to two, therefore, is impossible—is an absurdity—is *inconceivable :* no man can serve two masters.

On the next page, the resolution, they say, " puts into the mouths of all represented in this body a declaration of loyalty and allegiance to the Union and to the Federal Government.   But such a declaration, made by our members residing in what are called the seceding States, is treasonable." Treason is levying war against the government of one's country, or giving aid and comfort to an enemy carrying on war against one's country.   If, then, it is treasonable to profess fealty to the United States, the treason must be against another government—the C. S. A.   Here for the *third* time is the assumption that the rebellion is a government—a supreme, sovereign power.

On the preceding page there is another instance : " A man may conscientiously believe that he owes allegiance to one government or another."

Two supreme, sovereign powers are everywhere implied.

5th Case. (See Pr. Rev. for 1861, p. 558.)

" But suppose there is a difference of conscientious conviction among the members of the church as to the government to which their allegiance is due, what is the province' of the church in that case ?" Here again we have the idea of two supreme sovereignties claiming allegiance. Though not necessary to my logic, I stop to remark, that the exemplifications adduced by way of argument are entirely inapplicable. The question between the houses of York and Lancaster, between Charles I and the Parliament, between Orange and the Stuarts, and about the Salic law in Spain, were not at all questions of two supreme' governments, but simply which of two was the head of the one sovereignty of England or of Spain ; mere questions of succession.

6. (do., p. 562.) " Is not South Carolina a government ? Are not Georgia, Alabama, Virginia commonwealths ? " These brethren do not presume to say that the Assembly did not decide the question whether the allegiance of Presbyterians as citizens is due primarily to the several States to which they belong, or to the United States. The several States have constitutions and laws which

their citizens are sworn to support and obey. They are recognized in the Constitution and laws of the United States, by the Federal Government, and by all the nations of the earth. They are established, legitimate governments, to which allegiance, supreme or subordinate, is due. The answer, therefore, entirely ignores the real question in dispute. Its authors could not, of course, maintain that there was no difference of opinion among Presbyterians as to which of these governments, the State or Federal, they owe supreme allegiance. It is not correct, therefore, for them to say that the "Assembly has not determined, as between conflicting governments, to which our allegiance is due." This is the very thing they did decide. The Government of South Carolina is in conflict with the Government of the United States ; and the Assembly decided that Presbyterians in that State, and everywhere else in this country, are under obligations to strengthen, support, and encourage the Federal Government.

Observe here the gratuitous assumption that the Assembly decided against fealty to the State Governments. There is, however, no reference at all to State authorities in the resolutions; nor did they express the least doubt as to the obligations to the States' constitutions and laws, under the

United States Constitution and laws. Had the question of loyalty to the States' constitutions been up, there was not, probably, a single member of the body who would have hesitated a moment in giving an affirmative answer. Everybody knows that the Assembly would urge, as a *moral duty*, obedience to all legitimate State authority. But, as this idea was not before the house at all, it is more than illogical to assume that it was decided. It was, however, indispensable to their argument to have two governments to choose between, and they extemporize one out of a State, at the very moment when they admit that the State is not a government, has not a right to supreme allegiance, is not a power. The Government of South Carolina is in conflict with the Government of the United States, and the Assembly decided between them for the Presbyterian people. Reader! don't you see the false assumption that South Carolina is a supreme, sovereign power?

We must add, that the affirmation that all the nations of the earth recognize the States as separate governments, is both equivocal and untrue: equivocal, because it is doubtful, from the face of the sentence, whether it means a recognition of their existence as subordinate portions of the United States of America, or as independent

States; but in both senses it is untrue. No nation recognizes, in any legal way at all, any State separately. No man is known in Europe, or any other quarter of the globe, as a citizen of New Jersey, of Pennsylvania; but only as a citizen of the United States, resident in New Jersey, Pennsylvania, &c. No foreigner is ever naturalized a citizen of a particular State. No citizen travelling abroad ever applies to the consul of New Jersey, Pennsylvania, &c., for protection. But we must return.

The purpose logical for which this quotation is now made is perfectly accomplished; viz., to show that Dr. Hodge and friends do recognize the existence of two governments—the United States and the Confederate States of America. If the rebels could get as distinct a recognition from France and England, they would exult in the accomplishment of their secession and the establishment of their nationality.

7. I shall quote but one other case: The paper of the Kentucky Synod makes the same acknowledgment. It complains that the Assembly encouraged the people "to disregard the hostile governments which had been established over them, and, in defiance of actual authority of those governments, to pray for their overthrow. In the

judgment of a large minority of the Assembly, and of multitudes in the church, the subject matter of the action of the Assembly, being *purely political*, was incompetent to a spiritual court. Undoubtedly it was incompetent to the Assembly, as a spiritual court, to require or to advise acts of disobedience to actual governments by those under the power of those governments."

Here again, mark the full and distinct recognition of the independent sovereignty of the Confederate States of America. They are "*actual governments established over the people*"—"*those under the power of those governments.*" And this actual power is not an unlawful usurpation, but by actual AUTHORITY. Clearly, here is an acknowledgment of the Confederate States of America, and all the rebel States, as legitimate governments, having actual power and authority. My position is undeniably established; viz., that this ill-starred logic, all along, lays down as the basis of its argumentation and the corner stone of their system, the false position that the Confederate States of America is a *supreme, sovereign government*, to which the people of the South are bound to swear and maintain allegiance; *i. e.*, "the highest and greatest obligation of duty and obedience that can be," as Coke defines it, is due to the Confederate States of America.

Moreover, the Princeton Review admits the several States in rebellion to be governments. "Is not South Carolina a government? Are not Georgia, Alabama, Virginia, commonwealths?" Affirmative answer is indispensable to his argument; but this we cannot concede. True, in one sense, Virginia is a commonwealth; but so, Paul says (Eph. ii, 12), is the church of God—"the commonwealth of Israel." But will Dr. Hodge therefore affirm that the church is an independent, sovereign state, having Divine right to enforce civil allegiance from all within its bounds? South Carolina is *a* government, but only within the sphere marked out in her own constitution and that of the United States. This the Review expressly admits, in the very same paragraph: "They are established, legitimate governments, to which allegiance, supreme or subordinate, is due." Why say *supreme?* Because this is essential to his argument. But then it is notoriously untrue that the State Governments are supreme. Jefferson Davis had to blush to the lugs when he asserted this doctrine, and proved it by citing the second article of the Confederation, which expressly denies it and asserts the contrary.* No wonder, then, that the amiable and modest Review adds, "*or subordi-*

* See Appendix.

nate." This is true, but by no means justifies the *supreme,* which is notoriously untrue, but indispensable to be assumed in his argument. Here again we have the equivocal middle—true in one sense, false in another, and this *other* a *sine qua non* of the argument; which, therefore, is not an argument, but only a plausible sophism.

Thus our brethren acknowledge and declare the sovereignty and independence of the Southern rebellion !

But again, astounding as is this annunciation, they go much farther; *they decide a* PURELY POLITICAL *question.*

Toward the support of this allegation, remark, 1. The question whether a given people is a sovereign, independent nation, is surely *purely political.* It belongs to the very highest class of politics— the politics of nations. It is a question incapable of decision by any one nation. Is Liberia a nation? Does it stand, in the view of the world, an independent, sovereign power? Has it the right to declare war, conclude peace, coin money, make treaties, &c., &c.? Is not this political? Can any but the nations of the world decide it ? Does it not regard political relations solely? Most assuredly, the question of national sovereignty and independence lies in the higher regions of politics.

9*

It is not a question of morality simply, and of religion ; for the inhabitants of that region have long lived there under moral law and religious influences. They have long had churches and schools, and social order, and a government acknowledging itself subordinate to some other power. Now, is not the question of Liberian independence *purely political ?* Did our Government suppose itself intermeddling with morals and religion when it acknowledged the independent sovereignty of Liberia ? Well, then—

2. Our brethren, in affirming that the General Assembly decided, as between the two sovereign governments, the United States of America and the Confederate States of America, to which of the two Presbyterians owe allegiance, *did* decide, first, that the Confederate States of America is a supreme, sovereign power. It takes two to make a bargain ; and it takes two to make a choice. There is no choice possible, where there is but one object to choose between. Hobson's choice is simply no choice. "There's the horse," says John ; "you may choose out of my stable ; but your choice is limited to Dick." Before our brethren can make us decide, for Presbyterians, to which of two governments they owe " the highest and greatest obligation of duty and obedience that can be," they

must of necessity—a logical necessity, absolute and inevitable—present before us at least two objects of choice. This they have done in admitting the Confederate States of America to be a supreme, sovereign power.

But in doing this they have decided the highest purely political question. They have done precisely the thing which they charged us with doing. "They have digged a pit before me, into the midst whereof they have fallen themselves."

CHAPTER XXI.

THE DELIVERANCE OF THE GENERAL ASSEMBLY OF THE
PRESBYTERIAN CHURCH, 1862.

ON LOYALTY—THE BRECKINRIDGE PAPER.

The following paper, presented by Rev. R. J. Breckinridge, D.D., was adopted by a vote of 206 yeas and 20 nays, after full and extended discussion. It may be proper to state that of the twenty nays, all but five qualified their votes by sundry explanations in the form of dissents or protest; so that really there are on the record but five bold, unqualified negatives. The paper follows (see Minutes, 1862, p. 624):

"The General Assembly of the Presbyterian Church in the United States of America, now in session at Columbus, in the State of Ohio, considering the unhappy condition of the country in the midst of a bloody civil war, and of the church, agitated everywhere, divided in sentiment in many places, and openly assailed by schism in a large section of it; considering, also, the duty which this chief tribunal, met in the name and by the authority of the glorified Saviour of sinners, who is also the Sovereign Ruler of all things, owes to him our Head and Lord, and to his flock committed to our charge, and to the people whom we are commissioned to evangelize, and to the civil authorities who exist by his appointment; do hereby, in this deliverance, give utterance to our solemn convictions and our deliberate judgment touching the matters herein set forth, that they may serve for the guidance of all over whom the Lord Christ has given us any office of instruction, or any power of government.

" I. Peace is amongst the very highest temporal blessings of the church, as well as of all mankind; and public order is one of the first necessities of the spiritual as well as of the civil commonwealth. Peace has been wickedly superseded by war, in its worst form, throughout the whole land, and public order has been wickedly superseded by rebellion, anarchy, and violence, in the whole southern portion of the Union. All this has been brought to pass in a disloyal and traitorous attempt to overthrow the National Government by military force, and to divide the nation, contrary to the wishes of the immense majority of the people of the nation, and without satisfactory evidence that the majority of the people, in whom the local sovereignty resided, even in the States which revolted, ever authorized any such proceeding, or ever approved the fraud and violence by which this horrible treason has achieved whatever success it has had. This whole treason, rebellion, anarchy, fraud, and violence is utterly contrary to the dictates of natural religion and morality, and is plainly condemned by the revealed will of God. It is the clear and solemn duty of the National Government to preserve, at whatever cost, the National Union and Constitution, to maintain the laws in their supremacy, to crush force by force, and to restore the reign of public order and peace to the entire nation, by whatever lawful means are necessary thereunto. And it is the bounden duty of all people who compose this great nation, each one in his several place and degree, to uphold the Federal Government, and every State Government, and all persons in authority, whether civil or military, in all their lawful and proper acts, unto the end hereinbefore set forth.

"II. The Church of Christ has no authority from him to make rebellion, or to counsel treason, or to favor anarchy in any case whatever. On the contrary, every follower of Christ has the personal liberty bestowed on him by Christ, to submit, for the sake of Christ, according to his own conscientious sense of duty, to whatever government, however bad, under which his lot may be cast. But while patient suffering for Christ's sake can never be sinful, treason, rebellion, and anarchy may be sinful—most generally, perhaps, are sinful ; and, probably, are always and necessarily sinful, in all free countries, where the power to change the government by voting, in the place of force, exists as a common right constitutionally secured to the people who are sovereign. If, in any case, treason, rebellion, and anarchy can possibly be sinful, they are so in the case now desolating large portions of this nation and laying waste great numbers of Christian congregations, and fatally obstructing every good word and work to those regions. To the Christian people, scattered throughout those unfortunate regions, and who have been left of God to have any hand in bringing on these terrible calamities, we earnestly address words of exhortation and rebuke, as unto brethren who have sinned exceedingly, and whom God calls to repentance by fearful judgments. To those in like circumstances who are not chargeable with the sins which have brought such calamities upon the land, but who have chosen, in the exercise of their Christian liberty, to stand in their lot and suffer, we address words of affectionate sympathy, praying God to bring them off conquerors. To those in like circumstances, who have taken their lives in their hands and risked all for their country, and for conscience' sake, we say we love such with all our heart, and bless God such witnesses were found in the time of thick darkness. We fear, and we record it with great grief, that the Church of God, and the Christian people, to a great extent and throughout all the revolted States, have done many things that ought not to have been done, and have left undone much that ought to have been done, in this time of trial, rebuke, and blasphemy; but concerning the wide schism which is reported to have occurred in many Southern Synods, this Assembly will take no action at this time. It declares, however, its fixed purpose, under all possible circumstances, to labor for the extension and the permanent maintenance of the church under its care, in every part of the United States. Schism, so far as it may exist, we hope to see healed. If that cannot be, it will be disregarded.

"III. We record our gratitude to God for the prevailing unity of sentiment and general internal peace which have characterized the church in the States that have not revolted, embracing a great majority of the ministers, congregations, and people under our care. It may still be called, with emphasis, a loyal, orthodox, and pious church; and all its acts and works indicate its right to a title so noble. Let it strive for Divine grace to maintain that good report. In some respects the interests of the Church of God are very different from those of all civil institutions. Whatever may befall this or any other nation, the Church of Christ must abide on earth, triumphant even over the gates of hell. It is, therefore, of supreme importance that the church should guard itself from internal alienations and divisions, founded upon questions and interests that are external as to her, and which ought not by their necessary workings to cause her fate to depend on the fate of things less important and less enduring than herself. Disturbers of the church ought not to be allowed ; especially disturbers of the church in States that never revolted, or that have been cleared of armed rebels ; disturbers who, under many false pretexts, may promote discontent, disloyalty, and general alienation, tending to the unsettling of ministers, to local schisms, and to manifold trouble. Let a spirit of quietness, of mutual forbearance, and of ready obedience to authority, both civil and ecclesiastical, illustrate the loyalty, the orthodoxy, and the piety of the church. It is more especially to ministers of the Gospel, and, amongst them, particularly to any whose first impressions had been, on any account, favorable to the terrible military revolution which has been attempted, and which God's providence has hitherto so signally rebuked, that these decisive considerations ought to be addressed. And in the name and by the authority of the Lord Jesus, we earnestly exhort all who love God or fear his wrath to turn a deaf ear to all counsels and suggestions that tend toward a reaction favorable to disloyalty, schism, or disturbance, either in the church or in the country. There is hardly anything more inexcusable connected with the frightful conspiracy against which we testify, than the conduct of those office bearers and members of the church who, although citizens of loyal States, and subject to the control of loyal Presbyteries and Synods, have been faithless to all authority, human and Divine, to which they owed subjection. Nor should any one to whom this deliverance may come fail to bear in mind that it is not only their outward conduct concerning which they ought to take heed; but it is also and especially their heart, their temper, and their motives, in the sight of God, and toward the free and beneficent civil government which he has blessed us withal, and toward the spiritual commonwealth to which they are subject in the Lord. In all these respects we must all give account to God in the great day. And it is in view of our own dread responsibility to the

Judge of quick and dead that we now make this deliverance."

On this noble testimony to truth and loyalty I have little to say. The reader of this and the Spring resolutions will, of course, form his own opinion. He will undoubtedly perceive that, in comparison, the resolutions are mild and gentle— a portion of the lager beer of which the German laborer testifies, to prove its unintoxicating character, that he drank ten gallons and a half of it in one day ; and when the judge asked him how he felt, he replied, " I feels coote and I shleeps vel ; " and the Breckinridge paper is fourth-proof cognac, such as lost us the battle of Bull Run, July 21, 1861. If, therefore, the former were objectionable because they contained the decision of a political question, *a fortiori*, the latter is much more objectionable. This paper calls the secessionists "rebels." Is not this deciding a political question ? It affirms " a disloyal and traitorous attempt to overthrow the National Government by physical force." Is this no political question ? It decides on disloyalty and treason. " This whole treason, rebellion," &c.

" It is the bounden duty of all people who compose this great nation, each one in his several place and degree, to uphold the Federal Government and every State Government, and all persons in authority, whether civil or military, in all their lawful and proper acts." This is good mustard : the Spring resolutions in comparison are yellow cornmeal in a mustard bottle. No man can read the two articles without seeing, yea, *feeling*, that the action of the Assembly in 1862 far transcends in expansion, nerve, and vigor that of 1861 ; just as it should do to correspond with the changed state of the country at large. The Spring resolutions were opposed by sixty-six negatives to a hundred and fifty-six affirmatives. Had this paper of 1862 been supported by a feeble vote, the Southern secessionists, the cotton lords of Lancashire, and the London *Times* would have raised a shout of victory that would have gladdened the hearts of all the enemies of republican government throughout the world.

CHAPTER XXII.

A GOVERNMENT DE FACTO.

THE manner in which this later phrase has been used in this discussion, raises the suspicion that it is an instrument of error. What does it mean, and how does it become fallacious ?

De facto is simply *in fact—practical, actual.* In the phrase *a government de facto,* it implies a government—a power in actual exercise—in present operation. And the phrase is used for the purpose of ignoring the question of legitimacy. I enter a cotton mill and inspect the machinery : a gentleman takes me round, describes things as we pass on ; notices different operators ; gives a hint or a sign in one place, an express order in another. He is the governor *de facto ;* whether he is the owner I know not ; whether he has a *right* to direct these hands it is no part of my business to ascertain.

I visit a hospital : a gentleman in regimentals returns my salute and conducts me through the wards ; permits me to distribute tracts and Testa-

ments—to talk with the sick and wounded. I am
pleased and retire ; who the gentleman is I know
not ; whether he has authority to behave thus and
thus toward me and the invalid, is not a matter for me to inquire into—he is the *governor de
facto.*

I am sent by my government as an ambassador,
with letters addressed to his excellency Don Juarez,
President of the Mexican Republic. By the time
I arrive a revolution has taken place ; Juarez is
banished, a new regime is inaugurated ; I present
my credentials and am received, and treat with this
government *de facto*, without inquiring into the legitimacy of his authority ; that is a domestic matter with which I have no concern.

The French Revolution overthrew the Bour-
bons ; then came the reign of the people, then Napoleon, then Louis the Desired, then Louis Philippe. But the United States of America have no
difficulty in recognizing the government *de facto*,
and Louis Philippe had to pay indemnities occurring
under the administration of the preceding enemies
of his house.

Various contracts were entered into by the United States in Congress assembled, under the Articles : will they be binding under the Constitution ?
This question the fathers did not leave open, fear-

ing some difficulty about the *de facto* government ; but settled it in the Constitution.

In all the above changes, and even in the wars of the Roses in England, and the conflict between the Parliament and the Stuarts, the question never was raised, as between two governments, but, admitting always that the sovereignty is one and not diverse the sole *question* was wherein whose hands is the legitimate right of supreme rule ?

So in the secession of Absalom, there was no dispute about a government *de facto*. Such a dispute was impossible ; for there were not two governments. The sole controversy was about the deposit of the one supreme power. Is Absalom king, or is David king ? The idea of two supreme powers was not conceived as involved in that unhappy controversy.

In fact, this question of a government *de facto* is exclusively for a foreign power. It is always decided by a foreign power, and is simply a mode of expressing the idea of non-intervention of one nation in the interior concerns of another. Whether Louis Napoleon is legitimately in possession of the French throne, or Mr. Lincoln of the presidential chair, is not a question for England or Spain to decide. There is no room, therefore, for the *de facto* question in our case ; for there are not two claimants to the presidential chair. When the United States Government shall have been overturned—when Jefferson Davis shall have ousted all the present authorized agents of the people at Washington, and filled up the offices with the men of his own choice; when he shall have become the *locum tenens* of the White House, and claimant of sovereign power; then, and not till then, can the *de facto* question spring up; and then the governments of the world will have no difficulty in recognizing, as our brethren have done, the *de facto* government of the Confederate States of America. The slight change of the *United* into the *Confederate* will not long embarrass the powers of the world. But, until Generals Lee and Jackson shall have finished up their pleasure excursion to Harrisburg and Philadelphia, to New York and Boston, and erected the abomination that maketh desolate over Faneuil Hall and the granite stylus on Bunker Hill, the nations will not be called upon to encounter even this trifling embarrassment.

But our brethren use the *de facto* in quite another, and, as I must try to show, an illegitimate sense—the sense which Bull Run Russell inaugurated. Whenever a body of people separate and set up for themselves, and organize by the appointment of the officers by them deemed needful for the present, they have a government *de facto*. This, if I have been able to comprehend them (and I have labored to do so), is their idea. Here permit me to use the argument *ad absurdum*. If this assumption logically leads to grievous absurdities and fell ruin, then it must be abandoned as false. Such results as these following, must be met: viz., Absalom's was a government *pro tempore*, and ought to have been recognized as a government *de facto* by the nations. He organized his people—had all the necessary officers in his kingdom—had a larger number than David — he was a legitimate sovereign!

Robin Hood was a supreme and legitimate sovereign. His government was very energetic, and displayed many noble qualities. And so, every band of highway robbers or horde of pirates constitutes a government *de facto!*

Shays' rebellion, in Massachusetts, was a thoroughly organized company of intelligent, bold, and energetic men.

The whiskey insurrection in western Pennsylvania had less of organization, but they were organized. They had their squires and their captains, their companies and their regiment. So powerful and energetic was this *government de facto*, that Washington thought best to order out fourteen

10

thousand men to suppress it—one fifth of what President Lincoln ordered out at first to suppress the present insurrection—a vastly larger proportion than Mr. Lincoln's first levy.

Dorr's rebellion in Rhode Island was a still better organized movement. It included a body of legislative, judicial, and executive officers. Surely here was a government that ought to have been recognized as *de facto*.

The Southampton insurrection in Virginia was a very formidable affair. A large number of slaves associated together in the purlieus of the Dismal Swamp : they organized such a government as their capacity and circumstances called for. With their president at their head, who displayed great military and governmental ability, they became a terror to all the surrounding country. United States troops from Fortress Monroe and marines from two United States vessels were sent down to aid in suppressing this rising of some two or three hundred negroes. Now, according to the doctrine, Nat. Turner was a legitimate ruler, and his people ought to have been recognized as a government *de facto*—a nation !

But now the *reasoning* is identical, in all these cases, with that by which we are called upon to recognize the Confederate States of America as a government in fact. We all scout the conclusions, and thereby repudiate the premises. Neither Absalom nor Robin Hood, neither Shays nor Dorr, neither Tom the Tinker nor Nat. Turner nor Jefferson Davis is the head of a lawful government. Their efforts were, every one, insurrections and rebellions to put down a government.

But it may be said, If there is no recognition of them in any sense, how can this war end? How can you treat with them for its termination? I would say : As David treated with Absalom and his party ; the war is at an end as soon as the weapons of rebellion are cast down and the rebels return to their place in their country's government. "And Joab blew the trumpet, and the people returned from pursuing after Israel : for Joab held back the people." "And all Israel fled every one to his tent."

The fallacy, on this point, lies in using the word *government* sometimes in the lower meaning, as when we apply it to the management of a squad of soldiers or a school. In this low sense, I admit the Confederate States of America to be a government ; but the conclusion is deduced in the high and proper sense, as concerning a nation—a supreme, sovereign power.

CHAPTER XXIII.

REBELLION MAY EVENTUATE IN A SUPREME GOVERNMENT.

UNDOUBTEDLY, there is truth and justice in the adage, " Resistance to tyrants is obedience to God." In Chapter III, on Government, we have seen the foundation to be of Divine authority. If, then, civil government is an ordinance of God, how can resistance to it become a duty? If it be a solemn and religious duty to submit to the civil ruler as to a minister of God, how can rebellion ever be justified, and a rebel organization become a legitimate, sovereign power?

This question is of infinite importance. The ease and facility with which sophistry obscures it has made it one of great practical difficulty and danger. Upon the youthful mind of Virginia this sophistry has accomplished more delusion than, perhaps, any other. " Didn't our fathers rebel against England, throw off their allegiance, assert their independence, and vindicate it in a seven years' war?

And is not this their heroism the glory of America ? If they did right, can it be wrong for us to follow in their footsteps ? They were called *rebels*, and shall we shrink from the finger of scorn and an odious name ? " Thus the boys reasoned ; the fathers, many of them, knew not how to answer these sophisms, any more than the boys did — others, who saw the fallacy, gladly glossed it over, and led the boys on to slaughter.

The question before us is, *When* is rebellion justifiable ? If reason could have been brought to bear on the question, apart from passion, there would have been little difficulty in reaching a just and safe conclusion. This, however, could not be : passion ruled the fearful hour, and arrayed it in the terrors of a bloody conflict, and the boys and the sophists drifted to ruin.

We have seen that power to rule over men is God's ; that He has vested it in mankind ; that particular individuals can exercise it only by the consent of the ruled, expressed no matter how—by formal vote, by acquiescence, by silent assent ; that obedience to ruling authority, thus vested in magistrates' hands, is obedience to God ; and, *vice versa*, disobedience is rebellion against God. We have also seen that tyranny is no part of sovereign power—wicked, cruel, oppressive, brutal exactions have no divine sanction ; that these, persevered in, work a forfeiture of the legitimate powers, as in the hands of present rulers, and thus open the door for rebellion and make it right.

But the question springs up in our path, Who are to judge when and under what circumstances this forfeiture occurs ?—*when* the right to rule has reverted to the people, whence it came ; so that they are bound to resume its exercise and place it in the hands of other agents ?

Our answer is, The *people*—not a part, but the majority—must judge : they feel the oppressive burdens, and they only can judge of their weight ; but they must judge under a rule, according to truth. The rule, for a Christian people, is the word of God, and for us, besides, the Constitution of our Government. Accordingly, our fathers lay the basis of their Declaration on a few simple elements : " We hold these truths to be self-evident, that all men are created equal ; that they are endowed by their Creator with certain inalienable rights ; that among these are life, liberty, and the pursuit of happiness. That, to secure these rights, governments are instituted among men, deriving their just powers from the consent of the governed ; that, whenever any form of government becomes destructive of these ends, it is the right of the people to alter or to abolish it, and to institute a new government, laying its foundations on such principles, and organizing its powers in such form, as to them shall seem most likely to effect their safety and happiness." "But when a long train of abuses and usurpations, pursuing invariably the same object, evinces a design to reduce them under absolute despotism, it is their right, it is their duty, to throw off such government, and to provide new guards for their future security."

Here is the doctrine of truth and right. A government fails to secure to the people, life, liberty, and the pursuit of happiness ; but, on the contrary, unrighteously destroys life, rivets the chains of bondage upon the people, and turns their happiness into gall and wormwood : such rulers have forfeited their office, and may of right be hurled down from the seats of power.

A good example we have in the rebellion of the ten tribes against the house of David. The reason alleged was the heavy taxation under the splendid reign of Solomon. The glory of Israel as a kingdom was greatly advanced under this great scientific king ; but this involved great expense and heavy taxation. Upon the accession of Rehoboam, the people—a majority—made a strong remonstrance ; they appointed a grand committee of weighty men, who carried up their complaints and entreated a diminution of the taxes. This very reasonable request was rejected with insult, according to the counsel of the boys, "the young men which were grown up with him." (See 1 Kings, xii.) As might have been expected, the remonstrants became revolters, and set up the chairman of their committee as king of the ten or eleven tribes. Rehoboam levied an army of one "hundred and eighty thousand chosen men, which were warriors, to fight against the house of Israel." But this revolt was settled by another method. God sent his prophet to the king, saying, "Thus saith the Lord, ye shall not go up, nor fight against your brethren the children of Israel; return every man to his house: for the thing is from me." You have in the preceding chapter the reasons of all this. The grievous idolatry of Solomon (ver. 33) caused this revolt: "Because that they have forsaken me, and have worshipped Ashtoreth, the goddess of the Zidonians, Chemosh, the god of the Moabites; and Milcom, the god of the children of Ammon," &c. Therefore it was that God commissioned Jeroboam, the son of Nebat, to punish the house of David with this rebellion. Unfaithfulness to God leads to tyranny over men, and thus chastises itself. Yet this Jeroboam was even worse than Solomon and Rehoboam, and all the kings that followed ; so that his name became a proverb of malediction for wickedness: " Jeroboam, the son of Nebat, who made Israel to sin."

Thus a new kingdom is a result of rebellion on account of the abuse of power by heavy taxation ; and the declared purpose to go on and increase indefinitely the already intolerable burdens of the people. This new nation, however, had its origin farther back. For their gross idolatry, which is rebellion against their King, the nation of Israel were doomed of God to terrible chastisements, beginning in secession, and leading to never-ending wars between the nations of Judah and of Israel. For more than a thousand years these two powers were a scourge and a torment to each other. With a border line between them of less than a hundred miles, their conflicts were frequent and bloody ; their prosperity waned, their existence as separate nations was hardly recognized by the other nations, nor is there a single circumstance in their history to show that the rebellion of Jeroboam, the son of Nebat, was anything else but a curse of Heaven to punish for sin. That it would have been initiated by fearful slaughter, but for special and supernatural Divine interposition, the record expressly testifies. The army called out by Rehoboam to suppress

10*

the rebellion, "one hundred and eighty thousand men which were warriors," astonishes us. How such a body could be levied in so small a territory as the tribes of Judah and Benjamin possessed, it is difficult for us to conceive. Their whole territory was less than the State of New Jersey, and yet it turned out one hundred and eighty thousand men of war. Had President Lincoln ordered out at his first levy a million and a half, it would still have been a less proportion than swelled the armies of Rehoboam.

This rebellion resulted in an independent sovereignty, but by *express Divine command.* Such command is not to be expected in modern times. If, then, the King of all the earth is about to establish another power among the nations, His will must be ascertained in some other way. Rebellion —open and avowed hostility—direct resistance by a part of a nation against its government for its overthrow and utter subversion, so far as the rebellious portion is concerned—is another method of ascertaining a divine sanction for a new nation. The appeal to arms is an appeal to the Divine Being—the Lord of hosts, the God of battles. When our fathers took their cause up to this high tribunal, they presented to the world and recited before the Supreme Judge the reasons in its support. These cover the bulk of their immortal Declaration. They allege and prove a forfeiture, by the British crown, of all right of supreme sovereignty over these colonies, and affirm a reverting of the same to the people.

This is the issue joined, and the Great King and the Supreme Judge decided in their favor. And now that they have in a seven years' contest fought out the battle, and beaten down all opposition, the world of nations, acquiescing in the decision of the Supreme Judge, acknowledges these United States to be an independent, sovereign nation.

Such a movement our Southern people have inaugurated. Two things, therefore, they are bound to prove : 1st, that the sovereign powers vested in the United States have been forfeited by a cruel and tyrannical abuse, so that " life, liberty, and the pursuit of happiness " are no longer possible for the Southern people, under the United States Government, but " a long train of abuses and usurpations, pursuing invariably the same object, evinces a determination to reduce them under absolute despotism : it is their right, it is their duty, to throw off such government, and to provide new guards for their future security." 2d. They have to show their ability to vindicate sovereignty to themselves by arms, until opposition to their rebellion ceases, and this nation and the world acknowledges the fact of their independent sovereignty.

As to the first, there is scarcely a pretence—certainly not the shadow of any evidence—that the United States Government has, by tyranny, forfeited the right to rule. What is the government but the Constitution and the agencies it creates to execute it? That the country, the whole country, North and South, has prospered under it, no man pretends to deny—not even the most ultra secessionists. To evince the truth of this I cannot do better than to cite from Hon. A. H. Stephens's speech, delivered in the hall of the House of Representatives of Georgia, Nov. 14, 1860, in the presence of the members and of Hon. Mr. Toombs, and in reply to his speech. Not that Mr. Stephens is of authority, but because the matter he uttered on the point before us is true and defies the gainsayers. He responded most triumphantly to Mr. Toombs's objections in regard to the fishing bounties, the tariff, the navigation laws. After confuting him, he proceeds: "Now, suppose it to be admitted that all of these are evils in the system, do they overbalance and outweigh the advantages and great good which this same government affords in a thousand innumerable ways that cannot be estimated? Have we not at the South, as well as the North, grown great, prosperous, and happy under its operation ? Has any part of the world ever shown such rapid progress in the development of wealth, and all the material resources of national power and greatness, as the Southern States have under the General Government, notwithstanding all its defects ? " (Reb. Rec. I, 222.) * * * " There are defects in our government, errors in administration, and shortcomings of many kinds, but in spite of these defects and errors, Georgia has grown to be a great State. * * * There were many among us in 1850 zealous to go at once out of the Union, to disrupt every tie that binds us together. Now, do you believe, had that policy been carried out at that time, we would have been the same great people that we are to-day ? It may be that we would, but have you any assurance of that fact ? Would you have made the same advancement, improvement, and progress in all that constitutes material wealth and prosperity, that we have ?

"I notice in the Comptroller-General's report, that the taxable property of Georgia is $670,000,000 and upward, an amount not far from double that it was in 1850. I think I may venture to say that for the last ten years the material wealth of the people of Georgia has been nearly, if not quite, doubled. The same may be said of our advance in education, and everything that marks our civilization. * * * When I look around and see our prosperity in everything—agriculture, commerce, art, science, and every department of education, physical and mental, as well as moral advancement, and our colleges—I think, in the face of such an exhibition, if we can, without the loss of power, or any essential right or interest, remain in the Union, it is our duty to ourselves and to posterity to—let us not too readily yield to this temptation—do so. Our first parents, the great progenitors of the human race, were not without a like temptation when in the garden of Eden. They were led to believe that their condition would be bettered—that their eyes would be opened—and that they would become as gods. They in an evil hour yielded—instead of becoming gods they only saw their own nakedness.

" I look upon this country, with our institutions, as the Eden of the world, the paradise of the universe. It may be that out of it [the Union] we may become greater and more prosperous, but I am candid and sincere in telling you that I fear, if we rashly evince passion, and, without sufficient cause, shall take that step, that instead of becoming greater, or more peaceful, prosperous, and happy—instead of becoming gods, we will become demons, and at no distant day commence cutting one another's throats."

Such was the language of the most honest and talented Georgian, uttered not two years ago ; who would have supposed it possible that in less than three months the speaker would have himself become the Vice-President of these demons, and have inaugurated this throat-cutting process ! Alas ! into this "Eden of the universe" the incarnate fiend of secession had already entered, and up to this hour, Nov. 1, 1862, tens of thousands of noble men have been already offered up as victims at the accursed shrine of this Moloch !

Mr. Jefferson Davis, in his message of 29th April, 1861, is equally explicit in affirming the amazing prosperity of the whole South. He says [see Reb. Rec. I, p. 169] : "In the mean time, under the mild and genial climate of the Southern States, and the increasing care for the well-being and comfort of the laboring classes, dictated alike by interest and humanity, the African slaves had augmented in number from about six hundred thousand, at the date of the adoption of the constitutional compact, to upward of four millions.

"In a moral and social condition they had been elevated from brutal savages into docile, intelligent, and civilized agricultural laborers, supplied not only with bodily comforts, but with careful religious instruction, under the supervision of a superior race.

Their labor had been so directed as not only to allow a gradual and marked amelioration of their condition, but to convert hundreds of thousands of square miles of the wilderness into cultivated lands covered with a prosperous people. Towns and cities had sprung into existence, and rapidly increased in wealth and population under the social system of the South.

"The white population of the Southern slaveholding States had augmented from about 1,250,000 at the date of the adoption of the Constitution to more than 8,500,000 in 1860, and the productions of the South in cotton, rice, sugar, and tobacco, for the full development and continuance of which the labor of African slaves was and is indispensable, had swollen to an amount which formed nearly three fourths of the export of the whole United States, and had become absolutely necessary to the wants of civilized man."

Thus we have the testimony of the President and the Vice-President of the Confederate States of America, in proof of the great prosperity of the South, in every respect, under the protecting shield of the United States Government. Can any man believe that this prosperity accrued under a despotic power, so desperately cruel, unjust, and wicked, that resistance to it is obedience to God? On the contrary, this evidence is so conclusive in proof of the mildness, equity, and justice of the Government, that it is not necessary to proceed farther in support of the negative proposition, that the United States Government has not, by cruelty and oppression, forfeited its right to rule, and become, like George III, so despotic as to make resistance to the tyrant a duty. The speech of Mr. Stephens was delivered in the face of Mr. Toombs and the whole Georgia secessionists, and recites such evidences of prosperity as were undeniable, and, indeed, as were the boast and glory of the whole South, and are so at the present hour. The very epithet, KING COTTON, proves their own lofty conception of the vastness of their resources, the abundance of their wealth, and every other element of greatness, prosperity, liberty, and happiness.

Moreover, the idea of a forfeiture of sovereign rule and its return to the people in consequence, in a system which provides for that return once in every four years, is preposterous. Where is the sovereignty, the supreme, active sovereignty lodged ? Not in the President ; not in the Congress ; not in the judiciary ; not in the army ; not in the navy ; but spread all over. Its *semblance*, indeed, is in the President, but not its reality. And if it were, the South have had the supreme rule for forty-nine out of seventy-two years ; and the North twenty-three. Must the sovereignty be forfeited the moment it falls into Northern hands ? But it has never so fallen. Every presidential term it reverts to the people—not, indeed, to the people of South Carolina—of Virginia—of Pennsylvania—as, by a bloody fallacy, yet to be exposed, is assumed ; but to the PEOPLE of the United States, by whom the Government was established. These PEOPLE—not an insignificant fragment of them—but the PEOPLE of the United States, then appoint other hands to hold the power for a time : how then can it be forfeited ? The thing is impossible ; and, if you consider its division and partition to the other branches of the government—inconceivable. Such is the superhuman wisdom involved in this wonderful Constitution. Demonstrably evident, therefore, it is, that, as forfeiture is impossible, rebellion can never be justified. It must always and everywhere be a sin against that God who appoints the civil magistrate, and enjoins upon all men to obey him as his own minister, and assures us that they who " resist shall receive to themselves damnation."

The other point which the revolt must make out, before they become a nation, is the demonstration in blood. If they succeed—if they conquer the armies of the Republic—if they seize our fortresses

and our capital—if they carry on the war begun at
4 30 of April 12, 1861, by the first gun discharged
at Fort Sumter, until the United States surrender,
or cease the defence—if they fight on until the stars
and stripes are everywhere hauled down and trailed
in the dust, and the Government of the United
States say, It is enough—we yield and own you as a
nation—why, then, it will be even so ; and then
other nations may and will write the rebellion a success, and the result, one more added, by division, to
the family of nations. Whether this conditional
shall become an absolute proposition, is yet unre-
vealed. In the hands of an inscrutable Providence
the matter rests, and we must await the unrolling
of His scroll.

Meanwhile, I beg to add, by way of caution to
such as may be disposed to intermeddle : *Hands off!*
A title by prescription never accrues in the face of
an adverse claim, or against the commonwealth.

CHAPTER XXIV.

THE right of a people, when the form of their government becomes inefficient, oppressive, or in any way unsuitable, to alter and amend, or to abolish it and establish a new form, is everywhere admitted on this continent. The doctrine is prominent in position and in importance in the Declaration. No friend of freedom anywhere disputes it. God has deposited the supreme sovereignty in the people ; and government, which is their agency for its exercise, derives its just powers from their appointment or consent. Here we are all agreed.

But who are the people ? The term is manifestly vague ; and must be defined, if we use it in reasoning ; or then we must fall into error. For want of such definition, we meet with argumentation such as this : the people have an undoubted right to alter, amend, or abolish their government and form a new one ; therefore Virginia can go out of the Union and set up for herself, or form a new Union,

as she pleases.   And thus is demonstrated the right
and power of a part to destroy the building erected
by the whole.   The people formed the Constitution,
and surely they who made can unmake.   That is,
in one place the *people* means the citizens of the
whole United States ; in the other, the *people*
means the citizens of Virginia.   Now, the former
is true—the *people* of the United States established
the Constitution, and can at pleasure alter, amend,
or abolish it.   But it is not difficult to see that
the whole of a thing and one thirty-fourth or one
fourth part of that whole are not one and the self-
same thing.   The fallacy will be more palpable by
a full logical statement ; thus :

The people [of the United States] have a right
to alter the Constitution [of the United States].

But the inhabitants of Virginia are the people
[of the United States].

Therefore, the inhabitants of Virginia have a
right to alter the Constitution [of the United
States.]

The minor is false and the argument futile, and
yet it is one of the most popular and efficient of
these bloody fallacies.   I have seen it used often by
the soundest and clearest logicians in that State.
I have put in brackets the definitions : read without

them the fallacy is unseen, but with them the absurdity is at once exposed ; but when wrapped up in the loose verbiage of conversation or of stump oratory, it passes for overwhelming demonstration. " Are we slaves ? Are we tied down under bonds so that we can't alter our Constitution ? Are we not an independent, sovereign State ? And shall the free people of the Old Dominion—' the mother of States and of statesmen ' — be told that they haven't power to amend their Constitution, when they please and how they please ? What, then, have we gained by the Revolution, if we are thus cramped and held in ? " Thus it is that logic is crucified, and the blood of tens of thousands flows to amend the syllogism or to atone for its crucifixion.

A similar error is perpetrated upon the adopting act of the Virginia Convention. " We, the delegates of the people of Virginia, * * . * do, in the name and behalf of the people of Virginia, declare and make known, that the powers granted under the Constitution, being derived from the people of the United States, may be resumed by them whensoever the same shall be perverted to their injury or oppression." From these words the inference is deduced that the people of any one State— Virginia, *ex. gr.*—may withdraw, and resume the powers granted ; *i. e.*, may secede from the Union at pleasure. But the inference is a *non sequitur;* for the wording precludes it. The words set forth that the powers granted under the Constitution are derived from *the people of the United States;* secondly, that they may be *resumed* by *them.* By whom ? The people of Virginia ? Certainly not ; but by them by whom they have been granted—the *people of the United States.* Not by a *part*, a *portion*, a *fragment* of the grantors, but by the whole ; that is, by a majority. Whensoever the grantors—a majority of them—think proper, they can withdraw the powers, modify their exercise—alter and amend the whole instrument and the form of government which it establishes. This fallacy, whereby the term *people* is divided into two, and the argument spoiled by the creation of a fourth term, is identical with the preceding, in its substance. The extent of its range and the devastation it has spread over the land is inversely as the extent of space required for the exposure of its fallacious character.

CHAPTER XXV.

ALLEGIANCE, according to Lord Coke, is "the highest and greatest obligation of duty and obedience that can be." The word is of Latin origin, and signifies *binding to* the government—rather the king, ruler, emperor. It simply expresses the obligation under which the subject lies to obey and be faithful to his sovereign ; an obligation resulting not at all from his consent or his oath of allegiance, but from the providence of God, who placed the subject or citizen in that relation which the oath recognizes. So obedience, or true allegiance, borne to the sovereign is obedience to God. We are, accordingly, commanded to "submit ourselves to every ordinance of man, for the Lord's sake." "Command them to obey magistrates." All commands of the king, or sovereign power, not inconsistent with our duties to our Creator, are to be obeyed. But, should the supreme magistrate order the doing of anything contrary to God's law, we ought to obey God rather than man—we ought to obey the Supreme Lord rather than His erring minister, to whom He has never given authority to command and enforce obedience in doing a sinful thing.

Allegiance, it is thus evident, may be due and paid to the absolute Supreme and to the subordinate authorities too; but always having reference to the Supreme. Thus submission to the lowest civil officer, within his sphere, is obedience to God, and every intelligent Christian so views it, and thus brings the social, civil, and political duties of life within the sphere of morality and religion—God is in all his thoughts, and he honors Him in all his ways.

But if, in an evil hour, the magistrate order what God forbids, the question of allegiance springs up, as just stated—Whom shall we obey? To which claimant is allegiance due? Here there is no room for hesitancy. But when the claimants are fallible men, there may be practical difficulty, as in the case discussed in Chapters XVII, XIX, and XX. The principle on which the decision hangs is a question of authority—of moral power. Which of the two gives the clearest proof of a divine commission? In military affairs, when the first in command falls, the succession to the com-

11

mand is settled by *rank*. Or, if the major-general
is killed, and there yet remain two or more briga-
diers, the question is decided by *time*—the oldest
commission succeeds. In civil affairs, time and
rank are also elements ; but useful, as before, simply as indices of authority, pointing out the will of
the sovereign.

The question of allegiance, in all cases, resolves
itself into the question of supreme sovereignty. So
in the Revolution, our fathers first inquired into the
matter of forfeiture, and then pronounced the colonies "absolved from all allegiance to the British
crown." The supreme sovereignty thus reverted to
the United States in Congress assembled. Another
phase, however, of the question turns up in the
present rebellion, viz. : To which is the first allegiance due, to the State or to the United States ?
An erroneous answer to this dragged Virginia out
of the Union, and is rapidly converting the glorious
Old Dominion into an Aceldama. "My first allegiance is due to my State." This false assumption,
I do know, led many a pure and strong-minded man
into the midst of blood and carnage. Military re-
nown has followed ; but slaughtered thousands is
the price, and humanity and God will require an
account.

This proposition—"My first allegiance is due

to my State"—is an equivoke. There is a sense in which it is true, *i. e.*, chronologically. In the order of time it is true, but only in a reduced sense of the term allegiance. A correspondent of the New York *Times*, under date "Leesburgh, Va., Nov. 1, 1862," gives an excellent case for illustration of this, in relating a conversation with Hon. John Janney, into whose mouth he puts these words : "Sir, I am, in a word, a Virginian—a citizen of a commonwealth that had existed as a sovereign organized government for two hundred years before the United States had a name." "Such (the correspondent proceeds), in a sentence, is the history of the lapse of thousands of the best and purest men of Virginia—men who are now the mainstay of the rebellion in the council and in the field." Alas ! this record is true, and gives us another example of the fearful consequences of a lapse in logic. Where, now, lie the errors of this venerable, talented, distinguished, and patriotic man ? Primarily, in the assumption that Virginia was a sovereign State from the days of John Smith to the days of Thomas Jefferson. Two mistakes occur here. From the landing at Jamestown to the Declaration, by which the *United States* became the name of a nation, was only one hundred and sixty-nine years : this, however, is of no consequence to the argument. The first *fatal* error is the assumption that Virginia was all that time a "*sovereign*, organized government"; whereas, the radical and essential idea of a *colony* is, that it is a country cultivated by persons sent and coming from another country, under the care and protection of its government, and subject to its rule. Such was Virginia, all along, until 1776 : it never was a sovereign, but always a subordinate government ; and the most hearty and loyal to the British crown of all the colonies. Hence the very sobriquet, *Old Dominion*. (See *post.*, Chapter XV.) The other painful error is the assumption that his first allegiance is due to the State, as contradistinguished from the United States. Now, as I said, there is a sense in which, subordinately, it is true. In order of time—*before* the United States Government was established, allegiance, in a limited sense, was due the colonial government. But *first* is used here in another sense — *highest, greatest, most imperiously binding*. When a man affirms his first allegiance to be due to the United States, he means, not priority in time, but in degree, in magnitude—" the highest and greatest obligation of duty and obedience that can be." In this sense, the first allegiance is due to the United States ; the secondary and subordinate duty belongs to the State.

This is proved (1) by the nature of the thing. Allegiance is essentially the recognition of the supreme sovereignty and regulating the conduct in accordance with its nature. But it has been shown that no State in this Union ever was a supreme sovereign power : none ever pretended to set up such a claim, until Calhoun's rebellion began ; and to this day no power on earth has ever recognized any State as a supreme, sovereign power.

(2.) The Constitution explicitly and in the most express terms vests and recognizes the supreme sovereignty as existing in the United States Government. All the higher attributes of sovereignty belong to the United States, and not to the States. But, on the contrary, they are denied to the States. Art. vi says : " This Constitution and the laws of the United States which shall be made in pursuance thereof, and all treaties made, or which shall be made, under the authority of the United States, shall be the supreme law of the land ; and the judges in every State shall be bound thereby, anything in the constitution or laws of any State to the contrary notwithstanding." Now, on their own theory of a compact, the States all agreed to this article ; and on the theory of civil society being formed by voluntary agreement among the individuals composing it. This we have shown in Chapter I to be a baseless theory ; but if true, as assumed in the convention's letter, this wild scheme · of the greater allegiance being due to the lesser power, can never be defended. For, as the Convention says, " Individuals entering into society must give up a share of liberty to preserve the rest." This was done by the people when they " ordained and established this CONSTITUTION for the United States of America." This sixth Article was in it, and was accepted by all the States. Accordingly the next clause provides that " the Senators and Representatives before mentioned, and the members of the State Legislatures, and all executive and judicial officers, both of the United States and of the several States, shall be bound by oath or affirmation to support this Constitution." View the matter in every possible light, the evidence is conclusive that the highest allegiance is due to the highest power ; and every officer in every State has voluntarily sworn and subscribed to this doctrine, and promised " to support this Constitution."

(3.) But now this teaching of sound philosophy and of the Constitution is also the doctrine of the Bible. Rom. xiii, " Let every soul be subject to the higher powers,"—not to the *lower*, but the *higher*. Is the government of the nation, of the whole nation, established not by the people of a single State, but by the PEOPLE of all the States, as the *grand sovereign*—is this government a subordinate power; or is it the higher power to which all others are subordinate?

Again, 1 Pet. ii, 13, 14: "Submit yourselves to every ordinance of man for the Lord's sake; whether it be to the king, as supreme; or unto governors, as unto them that are sent by him for the punishment of evil doers, and for the praise of them that do well." Here the order of subjection is defined—the supreme, the subordinate: not *vice versa*, to the subordinate officer first and then to the supreme.

(4.) The Code of Virginia, published in 1860, prescribes the same order, p. 310. It states, in regard to officers elect, that before they enter upon official duties, they shall take the anti-duellist's oath; then the oath of allegiance to the United States Constitution; then the oath of allegiance to the commonwealth; then the oath of office. This is the order, and if any officer elect presumes to act officially, before he has taken these oaths, he is liable to fine and imprisonment.

Here, then, the Code of Virginia prescribes to all her officers to take the oath of allegiance to the Constitution of the United States first and foremost, and then to the State. Yet could tens of thousands of these sworn officers scout their oaths at the bidding of the arch traitor, and say with his subordinate, Mr. Thompson, "To Mississippi I owe *allegiance ;* and because *she* commands me, I owe *obedience* to the United States. But when she says I owe obedience no longer, right or wrong, come weal or woe, I stand for my *legitimate sovereign ;* and to disobey her behests is, to my conscience, treason." What a conscience ! that dictates obedience in the wrong as well as the right ! ! And what a reversal of reason, constitutional oath, and Scripture ! ! But here is the *fallacy ;* and nullification, secession, treason, and rebellion are the bloody results.

Let us pause a moment, for a glance at this new phase of patriotism ; for patriotic these men profess to be ; and vast numbers of them really believe their patriotism is of the true and genuine stamp. Let us analyze it. Patriotism is *love of one's country.* The word does not occur in the Bible ; hence it was alleged in debate last May, the church must not act on the subject. I think no one answered the argument. Probably it occurred to some, that the word grandfather is not found in the Bible, and therefore, though I may be under bonds to love my grandmother Lois, yet the old gentleman is not entitled to a share in my affections. Still it is more than probable that the commands to love our neighbor, to obey magistrates, to pay taxes, to live peaceably, to do good as we have opportunity, &c., cover the essence of patriotism. The question, however, springs up, when we define patriotism to be love of one's country, What is my country ? Is it the spot where I was born ? Now, I confess to local attachments. I travelled two hundred and thirty miles to preach on the seventy-first anniversary of my birth on the farm, and to sleep in the house in which I was born. Then and there I enjoyed a feast of melancholy but delightful reminiscences: and I will not deny that such local attachments are patriotic. But, if my soul could be shrivelled up to the limits of that farm, or even to those of East Pennsborough Township, Cumberland County, or even to the State of Pennsylvania, instead of patriotism, I should call it *mean selfishness.*

"Oh! once again to Freedom's cause return,
The PATRIOT TELL, the BRUCE of Bannockburn."

Did Tell bend his bow for Bürglen or for Switzerland ? Was his country Uri only, or the whole mountain holds of freedom ? Did Bruce fight at Bannockburn for Stirlingshire, or for the independence of Scotland ? Did the prince of Christian patriots draw his sword and fight his first battles

11*

for his native province, or for the defence of his majesty's American colonies ? Was Washington's patriotism limited to Virginia ? Was that his country which he loved ? Why, then, did he stay in the North, and there fight all his battles but one ? Why did he refuse to visit Mount Vernon and his native State for six long years, and even when Arnold was ravaging her coasts ? Clearly Washington's country, which he loved, for which he fought, for which he forsook Mount Vernon's peaceful shades, was not Virginia, but *United America*. His soul was incapable of such compression and condensation as that of the Mississippi representative or the great Southern sophist and nullifier.

Patriotism ! ay, such as cotton produces, this indeed cannot be found in the Bible ; but that love of country which the Revolution elicited, displayed, and illustrated—that love which discards the narrow limits of States and embraces the whole glorious Union—that love which took Washington to Boston, to Long Island, to New York, to Trenton, to White Plains, to Monmouth, to Brandywine, to Valley Forge, to Yorktown—that heroic, comprehensive patriotism may be found in the holy book wherever love to our neighbor is enjoined—wherever the gratitude of the heart is called forth toward any one who loveth our nation and hath built us a synagogue. As treason is the highest social and political crime, so patriotism is the highest social and political virtue.

CHAPTER XXVI.

SECESSION:

ITS FOUNDATION—SUICIDE—A BLOW AT CIVILIZATION—A SIN AGAINST REPUBLICANISM—CRUEL INJUSTICE—RIGHTS IN THE TERRITORIES.

SECESSION claims it as a right, under the Constitution, for any State to withdraw from the Union at pleasure ; and for reasons, if any at all, of which she is the sole judge. This is the doctrine, as drawn from Mr. Hayne by Mr. Webster, at the commencement of his unanswerable argument on that great occasion. The speech is one of the most illustrious triumphs of truth and logic over error and sophistry that occurs in the history of forensic or parliamentary discussion. It settled the question for almost a score of years, and it would have remained settled had not fanaticism and demagoguism formed a corrupt coalition, resulting in destruction to the peace of a continent—I may say the peace of the civilized world. Of course, there is no pretence set up here to amend the argument of the great expounder and immortal defender of the Constitution. But these brief chapters would lack an important link in their consistency and force, if this subject were omitted. It is proposed, therefore, to examine the theory of secession in a variety of aspects ; and, 1st, as to its foundation. The State, it is claimed, has the sole right to determine whether or not she has justifiable cause to secede ; and this is one of the reserved rights, which were never given up to the General Government.

But now, this reserved right is notoriously a wrong ; if the sentiments of all mankind, civilized and savage, are to be regarded. Surely there is no principle better and more universally settled in human judgment, than that a man is not a proper judge in his own cause. The converse principle subverts society, because it annihilates justice. If every man is to be judge in his own case, and " takes the law into his own hand," forms of justice vanish at once ; public order is impossible ; legislative, judicial, and executive powers are all reserved rights of the individual man. This is the halcyon return of the primeval state of insulation and individual independence—the enchanting savage state of primitive humanity. It is the very theory whose falsehood and absurdity we have exposed in Chapters II and III. There it is shown that man never existed, and never can, in such a state. God not only authorized, but organized society, and made every man his brother's keeper ; and Cain uttered a grievous falsehood when he denied it. " Am I my brother's keeper ? " Yes, you are. The supreme law of love, the sum of all law, binds every man that lives, and there is no escape from its obligations. His Creator lays them on, and no man can throw them off.

Nor let it be said, True, the individual man is not a proper judge in his own case, but the aggregate mass of a body politic are not so liable to err, and may with safety and propriety be its own judge of its own rights, and consequently of their infraction, and of their own course in the execution of their own sentence. This allegation assumes a point whose truth is at least not self-evident—that aggregate and heterogeneous masses, such as are found in every State, are better and safer judges than individuals. The contrary seems to me more like truth. A community is made up of individuals ; and how the selfishness and vicious passions, which pervert the judgment of all the individuals, are to be eliminated and lost in the aggregation, is not easily seen. More readily is it perceived, in the light of experience, that the disturbing elements in the way of a sound judgment are enhanced by their agglomeration. This is often exemplified in the declamations of the demagogue. If his audience is large, he is more likely to arouse their passions, and lead them to act contrary to sound discretion, than when he addresses a small number. Besides this natural tendency, there is great diminution of moral force in a divided responsibility. Men in associate bodies do things very often from which every individual would shrink were the whole responsibility laid upon himself. Many a false and unjust verdict has been awarded under the wrong and baleful influence of a supposed divided responsibility. Jurors erroneously imagine that but a twelfth part of the wrong verdict lies upon each, and, therefore, feel less of a burden on their shoulders than if each believed himself guilty of the whole wrong. So with other bodies of imperfect men. Evil passions multiply themselves in a geometrical, good, in an arithmetical ratio. These considerations make it exceedingly probable that a million of people, associated in a State Government, are at least as incompetent to be the supreme and exclusive judge in their own case as is the single individual.

Besides, there being no judgment possible, unless there be two things to be compared, there can be no judgment on any question of infraction of
. rights, unless there be two parties. If, therefore, one of the parties arrogate to itself the sole power

of determining when its rights are infringed, has the other party no rights ? Is it not equally entitled to decide the case ? Every State in the Union has equal rights ; and if one claims the right to judge that the Constitution has been violated to its injury, that decision is a charge of wrong doing against all the other States in union ; thus the one condemns the whole, but the right of the whole to form any judgment in the case at all, is denied ; and this is constitutional liberty and equality ! One thirty-fourth part has a right to charge and condemn the thirty-three thirty-fourths ; but the thirty-three thirty-fourths have no right to judge and condemn the one thirty-fourth ! ! And this is " equality among equals ! "

There is yet a second and more objectionable assumption here. It is assumed that this exclusive right of judging *when* there is good cause for seceding, is a reserved right to the States. But what says the Constitution ? Does it, indeed, make no provision for protecting the States and the people of the States ? Does it create no umpire and prescribe no remedy for State wrongs ? If an insurrection occur in any State, is there no provision for suppressing it by the power and at the expense of all the States—that is, at the expense of the United States ? If a revolution is gotten up in any

State, and the government is usurped by an arbitrary leader assuming monarchical power, does not the Constitution guarantee his dethronement and the continuance of a republican government ? And cannot the State claim and enforce the claim for its own protection ? Has not the Constitution created a judicial tribunal, with powers and duties to protect all individual citizens of all the States, in all their just rights, when State courts are incompetent to do it ? Did not the people in every State, and every State by the people, instead of reserving the right to judge in its own case, expressly concede the power to the United States? "In all cases, in which a State shall be a party, the supreme court shall have original jurisdiction." (Art. III, 2.) Thus the right of judging in all cases wherein a State is a party, is expressly granted to the United States, instead of being reserved, as secession maintains. So, to the States are guaranteed the right to recover, by United States authority and power, fugitives from justice and fugitives from labor. The States thus expressly concede this power to the United States. Utterly groundless, therefore, is the assertion that the State is the sole and exclusive judge of its own wrongs, and *when* they amount to a just cause of secession. The Constitution furnishes the most safe, because the most impartial tribunal conceivable, to meet these very cases, and every State has conceded this to the Union.

(3). A third stone in the foundation of the right of secession, is, that the States were sovereign powers—separate nations in fact. This we have shown is not so—never was so. (Chap. VI.)

(4). A fourth is, that the States were independent, *severally*, at the Declaration. This we have also proved to be utterly a mistake. See, in Chaps. XIV and XV, the testimony of the leading Southern men, especially those of South Carolina, against this " political heresy," as Gen. Pinckney calls it.

(5). That the Constitution created a confederation—that it is a compact merely—is the fifth item in the basis of secession. This has been disproved, we hope, abundantly, in Chap. XII, where it is made evident that the question, whether to establish a *government* or to amend and perpetuate the *confederation*, was *the* question most discussed, and most warmly ; and when the advocates of a government and opponents of a confederacy gained the day, the agony was over ; there remained no dangerous rocks in the current of their legislation—save only the slavery question.

(6). A sixth rotten sandstone in this foundation, is the doctrine that a man's first allegiance is due to the State, and a secondary allegiance only is due to the United States. This has been refuted in Chap. XXV.

(7). That the Constitution was adopted by the States, as organized governments, and not by the people, is another foundation—a mere cobble stone it is, as is shown in Chap. XI—where the sophism of Calhoun, as reiterated by Mr. Jefferson Davis, is stripped of its power to deceive.

All these seven are necessary and constitute the substratum on which the structure of secession rests. None of them can be spared or the building cannot stand; and as they are every one untrue, the superstructure is doomed to an early fall, and the ruin of that house must be great and irremediable.

II. The right of secession is a stupendous wrong, inasmuch as it is the right to commit suicide. A nation that embodies this supposed principle as a part of its fundamental law, provides for and secures its own destruction. A reserved right to withdraw from any association without reason rendered, is a right to dissolve it at pleasure; and this may be practicable, and perhaps prudent, in such associations as are indifferent in themselves as to whether they exist or not. Where the object of association is a matter morally indifferent, and there is no obligation, no moral necessity for its existence, this may be allowed. But as human society and government are ordinances of God, and indispensable to human existence, the power of self-destruction is not allowable. No individual has such a moral power. The argument of the suicide is fallacious. He argues thus : Whatever is my own I may dispose of at pleasure ; but my life is my own ; therefore I may dispose of it as I please ; and inasmuch as life has become a burden and a weariness, and not a blessing, I choose to lay it aside. But here are two false assumptions. It is assumed that a man may dispose of his property as he pleases. This is not true. No man has a right to burn his house, to kill his horse, to throw his bank notes into the fire, or his silver and gold into the ocean. " The silver and the gold are mine, saith the Lord of hosts "— worldly goods are gifts—rather loans from our Supreme Lord, and we have no right to use them but for His glory and the good of men. The other error is, that a man's life is his own. It is not so. It belongs to God, and must be used for the same end.

Now, as with the individual, so is it with society—with government ; the right of self-destruction is a nullity—a murderous wrong. In Chap. I we have seen in what sense expatriation is a right and a duty, viz., as a removal from one country and government to another, when the general welfare will be promoted ; but from human society no man has the right and power to remove.

The Duke of Argyle, in one of the very first speeches uttered by any man of distinction in Britain that does justice to America, remarked : " We will not regard the question, of what is called the right of secession ; no government has ever existed, to my knowledge, admitting the right of separation within itself. There is a curious kind of starfish in the waters of Loch Fine, which I myself have caught several times, and which effects the most extraordinary and adroit species of suicide. On drawing it from the water and attempting to remove it from the hook, the fins immediately drop off, the body falls in pieces, and of one of the most beautiful forms of nature, nothing remains but a few fragments. Such would have been the fate of the American Union, had its Government accepted what is called the right of secession. Gentlemen, we must admit in all justice, with respect to Americans, that they are fighting for things that are worth the pains, and that the national existence is one of these things." Count de Gasparin adds : " Yes, the national existence. This idea alone contains the unanswerable refutation of what is called the right of secession. But is a confederation a nation? Is it not rather an assemblage of nations? We are reminded of the celebrated definition of Montesquieu : ' A community of communities.' "

Count Gasparin proceeds to remark on our government as such, and that it is not a confederation ; and comes very near stating the doctrine we have defended and illustrated in Chap. XII, viz., that a federal government—meaning by government an independent, sovereign nation—is a moral impossibility, as well as a logical contradiction.

III. This doctrine is a blow at all social organization. If there exist a right for a State to withdraw from the Government of the United States, the same right exists in a county to withdraw from the State, a township or borough from the county, the family from the town, the wife from the husband, and the children from the family. It is a perfect disintegration, and leaves nothing of the beautiful starfish but a few insulated fragments of humanity. When I used this argument in public debate with secessionists in Virginia, I was met by this response : " No, because the county is not a sovereign power." My obvious and unanswered rejoinder was, Neither is a State—never was—never supposed itself to be a sovereign nation. No people

on earth ever recognized any State as a sovereign
nation. Thus the abstract argument stands unas-
sailed and unassailable. It runs the doctrine into
an inadmissible absurdity, but it does it logically.

But this absurd result of the doctrine is not an
abstraction. I met it in the concrete often in
1848–'55 in Washington College, Va., where it had
broken the arm of discipline. Often, often have
students, who, from negligence of study or vicious-
ness of conduct, had reason to apprehend the ap-
proach of the amputating instruments, come to me
and informed me they wanted to *resign*. It was to
me a strange language, and it required time and
attention to ascertain its true intent and meaning.
It turned out that the object was to escape discipline, by cutting the bond of connection and
throwing themselves beyond the limits of college
authority—they claimed the right of secession.
This is a single illustration of the principle ; but
thus the foundations are destroyed everywhere. The
offender against law—any law, school law, church
law, civil law, all law—has only to throw himself
upon his reserved right and say—I secede : now he is
outside of your jurisdiction, and ruling power is
prostrated : government is at an end. Mine eyes
run down with tears because " they have made void
thy law."

IV. Secession is, of course, a sin against republican government. It would be difficult to conceive more favorable circumstances under which to try the experiment of man's self-government, than we have had. The planting of the colonies in their different locations—their growth up under necessities most imperiously demanding their utmost prudence and greatest energies toward self-support—a hundred and seventy years' training in this school of necessities, by which the people, individually and aggregately, were constrained to call forth all their powers—the very difficulties which, toward the close of this long schooling, sprung from the blundering management of the British ministry—the diplomatic tact which in a ten years' effort by negotiation to adjust these difficulties was acquired by the leading statesmen of the republic—the large amount of true, honest, Christian patriotism, which leavened the entire mass of the people—all these seem to put off to a distant day any hope of a more favorable experiment. If, therefore, this fail, as secession insures its failure, man may give over as hopeless all government by the people ; and fall back upon despotic power as the only alternative for the race.

V. Secession is unjust. This has been pointed out a thousand times. The territories purchased by the United States have, to a large extent, been formed into States, as Louisiana, Florida, Texas; and vast millions besides the purchase money have been expended in removing the Indians, in building fortifications and lighthouses. And yet secession carries all this out of the Union: a small portion of the people who made the purchase, &c., carrying off the whole. The iniquity is glaring.

Again: Suppose Pennsylvania secedes—and, of course, she has equal rights with other States—her territory cuts the United States in two, extending as it does from Lake Erie to the seaboard, or nearly. After seceding, she makes herself a province of the British empire, and, of course, becomes a most efficient foe of the United States, in case England makes war upon them. The iniquity of this is easily perceived, but cannot at all be estimated.

VI. Secession, we have just seen, has no solid ground to stand on. One alleged ground we have yet to notice—*equal rights in the Territories*. This, it is said, is denied by the United States. Mr. Lincoln's election, says Rev. Dr. Thornwell, of South Carolina, changes the government fundamentally—it is a revolution in the government. The only reason this ablest advocate of secession lays down for it, is the exclusion of the South from the Territories. And yet there was no such exclu-

12

sion before the rebellion. There was not a foot of territory in the Union from which the slaveholder was excluded by any act of the Government. Nature sets up a barrier. Frost and snow are not congenial to the colored people; and this is the only exclusion: but legislation has thrown no obstacle in the way; and judicial decisions have declared equal access to the slaveholder and his property, as to the non-slaveholder.

But, however this may be—and we cannot *discuss* the subject—one thing is plain—that it is a merely abstract question. Concede equal rights in the Territories, does any slaveholder wish to go thither? Is there any place where slavery can be profitably planted? These gentlemen themselves respond in the negative. They know perfectly well that Kansas is impracticable to the peculiar institution. If it were perfectly open to-day, no Southerner would remove into it. Hon. R. J. Walker, in his letter to President Buchanan, made this perfectly plain. Is it wise, we ask, is it prudent, is it Christianlike, to baptize a continent in Christian blood for a bald abstraction? Decide the question whichever way you please, the practical results are the same. Slavery can never go where it is unprofitable, and we have no territory in which it would be profitable. Should it be said we may acquire such hereafter, this, too, is practically an abstraction ; for, if the right were admitted, then, in case the question should arise of taking in new territory suitable for slave culture, the pros and the cons would try their strength on this previous question. The slave interest would vote for taking in, and the free against it. Long since, Mr. Clay attempted to prove, and, it seemed to me, did prove, that northern Texas could not ultimately be slave territory. It is large enough for two States, which must necessarily be devoted to the product of cereal crops, by the culture of which slaves cannot support themselves. Mr. Calhoun, in conversation with the present writer in 1845, stated that he was too far north—in Abbeville District, South Carolina—for the profitable working of his people in the production of cotton ; that he had removed a part of them to Alabama, where his son, as partner with him, was planting ; and that, as soon as he could make the arrangements to suit, he would remove them all to the more congenial clime. Why, then, fight against nature, and distract the world for a bald abstraction ?

CHAPTER XXVII.

FUGITIVES FROM LABOR.

RIGHT IN LABOR RECOGNIZED—COTTON GIVES IT VALUE—IN-
TERCHANGE OF OPINION, NORTH AND SOUTH—HISTORY OF
KING COTTON—SLAVE-TRADE EXTENSION—RENDITION DUTY
OF STATES—PREDICTION OF RUIN FROM SLAVERY AGITA-
TION—WRONG-DOING NORTH—NO JUSTIFICATION OF SECES-
SION—SECESSION NO REMEDY—DIFFICULTY OF RENDITION.

THERE can be no controversy as to the recognition, by the United States Constitution, of a right
of property in man's labor. Article IV, section 2,
clause 3 : "No person held to service or labor in
one State, under the laws thereof, escaping into
another, shall, in consequence of any law or regulation therein, be discharged from such service or
labor, but shall be delivered up on claim of the
party to whom such service or labor may be due."
Whatever opinions may be held, as to the abstract
question of slavery, in a moral point of view, there
can be but one opinion as to the recognition of its
existence in the country, and under the Constitution. Service or labor may be due, that is, *due* by

the laws of one State ; and the design of this clause
is to secure this due service.

Slavery, or, in Southern phrase, "the peculiar
institution of the South," was viewed by the fathers
as an economic evil, and by many as a moral evil;
and the idea of its abatement was very generally
held, even in the South.   It cannot be disputed—
and we believe it is not, except by a very few ultra-
ists—that, until a recent period—until Whitney's
cotton gin made it profitable—the idea of its perpetuity and extension was not held and advocated
by any of the great statesmen even in the South.

The history of cotton is a history of this change
of opinion.   A few weeks before his inauguration,
Washington wrote to his intended secretary, Hamilton, and proposed the question whether, constitutionally, a bounty could be offered by Congress on
hemp and cotton.   He expressed the hope and belief that both these articles might be produced in
our country, and the opinion that it would be sound
policy in the Government to foster their production
by bounties.

With this introductory remark, we present the
following, from Mr. Everett's address in New York,
published as an introduction to the Rebellion Record. See vol. i, p. 29.

" But the history of the great Southern staple

is most curious and instructive. His Majesty, 'King Cotton,' on his throne, does not seem to be aware of the influences which surrounded his cradle. The culture of cotton, on any considerable scale, is well known to be of recent date in America. The household manufacture of cotton was coeval with the settlement of the country. A century before the pianoforte or the harp was seen on this continent, the music of the spinning wheel was heard at every fireside in town and country. The raw materials were wool, flax, and cotton, the last imported from the West Indies. The colonial system of Great Britain, before the Revolution, forbade the establishment of any other than household manufactures. Soon after the Revolution, cotton mills were erected in Rhode Island and Massachusetts, and the infant manufacture was encouraged by State duties on the imported fabric. The raw material was still derived exclusively from the West Indies. Its culture in this country was so extremely limited and so little known, that a small parcel sent from the United States to Liverpool in 1784 was seized at the customhouse there as an illicit importation of British colonial produce. Even as late as 1794, and by persons so intelligent as the negotiators of Jay's treaty, it was not known that cotton was an article of growth and export from the United States. In the twelfth article of that treaty, as laid before the Senate, cotton was included with molasses, sugar, coffee, and cocoa, as articles which American vessels should not be permitted to carry from the islands, or *from the United States*, to any foreign country.

"In the revenue law of 1795, as it passed from the House of Representatives, cotton, with other raw materials, was placed on the free list. When the bill reached the Senate, a duty of three cents per pound was laid upon cotton, not to encourage, not to protect, but to create the domestic culture. On the discussion of this amendment in the House, a member from South Carolina declared that 'cotton was in contemplation' in South Carolina and Georgia, 'and, *if good seed could be procured, he hoped it might succeed.*' On this hope the amendment of the Senate was concurred in, and the duty of three cents per pound was laid on cotton. In 1791, Hamilton, in his report on the manufactures, recommended the repeal of this duty, on the ground that it was 'a very serious impediment to the manufacture of cotton;' but his recommendation was disregarded.

"Thus, in the infancy of the cotton manufacture of the North, at the moment when they were deprived of the protection extended to them before the Constitution by State laws, and while they were struggling against English competition under the rapidly improving machinery of Arkwright, which it was highly penal to export to foreign countries, a heavy burden was laid upon them by this protecting duty, to enable the planters of South Carolina and Georgia to explore the tropics for a variety of cotton seed adapted to the climate. For seven years, at least, and probably more, this duty was, in every sense of the word, a protecting duty. There was not a pound of cotton spun, no, not for candle wicks to light the humble industry of the cottages of the North, which did not pay this tribute to the Southern planter. The growth of the native article, as we have seen, had not in 1794 reached a point to be known to Chief Justice Jay as one of actual or probable export. As late as 1796, the manufacturers of Brandywine, in Delaware, petitioned Congress for the repeal of this duty on imported cotton, and the petition was rejected on the report of a committee, consisting of a majority from the Southern States, on the ground that 'to repeal the duty on raw cotton would be to damp the growth of cotton in our own country.' Radicle and plumule, root and stalk, blossom and boll, the culture of the cotton plant in the United States was in its infancy the foster child of the protective system.

"When, therefore, the pedigree of King Cotton is traced, he is found to be the lineal child of the Tariff; called into being by a specific duty; reared by a tax laid upon the manufacturing industry of the North, to create the culture of the raw material in the South. The Northern manufacturers of America were slightly protected in 1798, because they were too feeble to stand alone. Reared into magnitude under the protective system and the war of 1812, they were upheld in 1816 because they were too important to be sacrificed, and because the great staple of the South had a joint interest in their prosperity. King Cotton alone, not in his manhood, not in his adolescence, not in his infancy, but in his very embryo state, was pensioned upon the treasury—before the seed from which he sprung was cast in 'the lowest parts of the earth.' In the book of the Tariff 'his members were written, which in continuance were fashioned when as yet there was none of them.'

"But it was not enough to create the culture of cotton at the South, by taxing the manufacturers of the North with a duty on the raw material; the extension of that culture, and the prosperity which it has conferred upon the South, are due to the mechanical genius of the North. What says Mr. Justice Johnson, of the Supreme Court of the

12*

United States, and a citizen of South Carolina?
'With regard to the utility of this discovery (the
cotton gin of Whitney), the Court would deem it a
waste of time to dwell long on this topic. Is there
a man who hears us that has not experienced its
utility ? The whole interior of the Southern States
was languishing, and its inhabitants emigrating, for
want of some object to engage their attention and
employ their industry, when the invention of this
machine at once opened views to them which set
the whole country in active motion. From child-
hood to age, it has presented us a lucrative employment. Individuals who were depressed in poverty
and sunk in idleness, have suddenly risen to wealth
and respectability. Our debts have been paid off,
our capitals increased, and our lands trebled in
value. We cannot express the weight of obligation which the country owes to this invention ; the
extent of it cannot now be seen.' Yes ; and when
happier days shall return, and the South, awaking
from her suicidal delusion, remembers who it was
that saved her sunny fields, with the seeds of those
golden crops with which she thinks to rule the
world, she will cast a veil of oblivion over the
memory of the ambitious men who have goaded
her to the present madness, and will rear a monu-
ment of her gratitude, in the beautiful City of

Elms, over the ashes of her greatest benefactor—
ELI WHITNEY."

A similar change of sentiment occurred in the
North. It is undeniable that the extension of time
for the toleration of the slave trade, from 1800 to
1808, was effected by the Northern vote. It stood
thus : yeas, New Hampshire, Massachusetts, Connecticut, Maryland, North Carolina, South Carolina,
and Georgia—7 ; nays, New Jersey, Pennsylvania,
Delaware, and Virginia—4. A change of sentiment, therefore, has come over the spirit of the
Northerners, analogous, but counter to the subsequent change South, mentioned above. But the
Constitution remains unchanged, and to attempt its
change by forced interpretation is disingenuous and
dishonest.

A fair and candid construction of this rendition
clause, in our opinion, makes it the duty of the
State to which the fugitive " flees " or " escapes "
to deliver him up. In hermeneutics the law is settled ; words and phrases occurring in different parts
of the same instrument of writing, are to be understood in the same sense, unless there be some insu-
perable objection. If this rule is abrogated, all certainty in the use of language becomes impossible,
and written agreements indefinite and vague ; and
written constitutions have no advantage over the

lex non scripta of the British Constitution. Assuming the stability and truth of this rule, we remark that the phrase, " shall be delivered up,"
which occurs in this clause, occurs also in clause
second ; the person fleeing from justice " shall be delivered up ;" the person " escaping from such service or labor " " shall be delivered up." Neither
clause expressly defines by what power or authority
the delivery up shall be effected. But clause second says, on demand of the executive authority of
the State from which he fled, the fugitive " shall
be delivered up, to be removed," &c. Construction,
however, has settled the meaning to be, that the
delivery up of the alleged criminal shall be by the
executive of the State to which he fled ; and Governor Packer, of Pennsylvania, so construed the
Constitution, when he arrested Cooke, and wrote to
the Governor of Virginia to send for him. Now,
give the same exact interpretation to clause third,
and it becomes the duty of the executive of the
State to which he escapes, to deliver up the fugitive from service or labor. In clause second, the
claim for the fugitive is made by the party concerned, viz., the executive, as the head of the State
against whom the offence has been committed : so
in clause third, the claim is made by the party to
whom the service or labor is due ; and assuredly

the response to that claim ought to be made by the executive of the State to which the fugitive escaped. Had this plain meaning of the Constitution been carried out in practice, there is a high probability that the present civil war would not have fallen out. On this topic I crave the reader's pardon for introducing a part of a speech delivered in the Synod of Cincinnati in the year 1843, and now out of print, on the occasion of the very improper introduction, as I thought it, of the slavery controversy into that body. The speech occupied over eight hours in the delivery, and a part of it, containing the Bible view of slavery, was printed forthwith, from the first hasty notes. The extract is inferentially prophetic. The reader will judge how far the prophet was inspired with the afflatus of a true deductive logic. The latter part of the prediction I hope and believe will not be altogether fulfilled and verified by history. It is a little exaggeration, thrown in with the view and hope of rendering the whole a prophylactic remedy for a fearful evil, seen in the dim distance. "Should the opposite doctrine prevail—should the holding of slaves be made a crime by the officers of the churches—the non-slaveholding States, should they break communion with their Southern brethren, and denounce them as guilty of damning sin, as kidnappers and menstealers, as worthy of the penitentiary, as has been done here in this Synod—should this doctrine and this practice prevail throughout the Northern States, can any man be so blind as not to see that a dissolution of the Union—a civil and perhaps a servile war must be the consequence ?—such a war as the world has never witnessed—a war of uncompromising extermination, that will lay waste this vast territory, and leave the despotic powers of Europe exulting over the fall of the Republic ? All the elements are here—the physical, the intellectual, the moral—elements for a strife different in the horribleness of its character from anything the world has ever witnessed. Let the spirits of these men be only once aroused ; let their feelings be only once chafed up to the fighting point ; let the irritation be only kept up until the North and the South come to blows on the question of slavery, their 'contentions will be as the bars of a castle,' broken only with the last pulsations of a nation's heart."

"On the contrary, let the opposite doctrine prevail, and the practices which necessarily flow from it—let the North pity their Southern brethren who are afflicted with slavery—let the churches of the North deal kindly and truly with the South —let them continue to recognize and treat them as

Christians, and entreat them and urge them to give unto their servants that which is just and equal, to treat them as Christian brethren—let them aid them in the splendid scheme of colonization—let them seek union, and peace, and love, and they will not seek in vain. Thus, the integrity of the nation will be maintained. The happiness of the colored race will, in the highest degree, be promoted, in the land of their fathers' sepulchres. God will be glorified in the triumphant success of free, republican America."

But be this question answered as it may—be the power of delivering up the fugitive from labor lodged either in the State authorities or the United States, the duty of executing this clause lies somewhere, and the corresponding right is indubitable. Equally undeniable is the fact, that this right has been imperfectly vindicated, and hence the South has just cause of complaint. Be the obstructions, intentionally thrown in the way of rendition, from what source or of whatsover character they may, whether from interference, aiding the escape or concealing the runaway, or preventing the officer of the law from performing his duty ; or from State legislation, or from defects in the United States' legislation and the failure of United States officials in the execution of the laws—all such obstructions and avoidable failures are a violation of the plain letter of the Constitution, and have a natural, strong, and direct tendency toward a dissolution of the Union.

Nevertheless, while all these obstructions are worthy of the most severe reprehension in themselves, and on account of their tendency to weaken the bonds of our nationality, yet must we think their real and actual influence was far from being a justifiable cause of dissolution. Rather were they a pretext seized upon to justify a foregone conclusion, deduced from far different premises.

The first ground of this last opinion lies in the fact, that the United States Government never refused to exert its power; and, as President Buchanan states in his last annual Message, it never failed in a single instance, when seasonably applied to, to execute the fugitive slave law. Why, then, should the South aim a blow at the United States, as though it had been derelict in regard to this constitutional duty ?

But a second reason is, that the States whose citizens lost many servants were not the leaders in this rebellion. Not Delaware, not Maryland, not Virginia, not Kentucky, not Missouri, but South Carolina took the lead ; South Carolina, whose citizens lost nothing. On this point let me be again indebted to Mr. Everett :

" The number of fugitive slaves, from all the States, as I learn from Mr. J. C. G. Kennedy, the intelligent superintendent of the census bureau, was, in the year 1850, 1,011, being about one to every 3,165, the entire number of slaves at that time being 3,200,364, a ratio of rather more than one-thirtieth of one per cent. This very small ratio was diminished in 1860. By the last census, the whole number of slaves in the United States was 3,949,-557, and the number of escaping fugitives was 803, being a trifle over one-fiftieth of one per cent. Of these it is probable that much the greatest part escaped to the places of refuge in the South, alluded to before (the Dismal Swamp, the everglades of Florida, the mountain regions, the Mexican States, and the Indian territory). At all events it is well known that escaping slaves, reclaimed in the Free States, have in almost every instance been restored."

Another evidence arises from the inefficiency of secession, as a remedy against the loss of servants by flight. If these losses are unendurable, even with the whole power of the United States exerted to prevent them, what will they not be if this power withdraws its protection, and leaves the hostile feeling toward slavery, under all the aggravations of a bloody civil strife, to goad on the work of running off negroes, along a boundary line of twenty-five or thirty hundred miles? This is the boundary which secession claims between freedom and slavery; and how is it to be guarded? Plant forts on or near to the line at the distance of five miles apart; and place in each fifty soldiers as sentinels to guard the way against fugitives, would your five hundred forts and your twenty-five thousand sentinels be able to prevent the negro's escape? Could they operate the hundredth part of the influence which is now exerted by the United States authorities? Why, the very fact of such a guard would inspire the negro with intensely increased desire to escape and courage to make the attempt; and at the same time it would stimulate to redoubled efforts, all along the line, those on the free side who would be ready to afford every facility to escape. Besides, the moment the slave crosses the line, the sentinels of the masters dare not step across to follow him. That would be an aggression, and would be instantly resisted. And this suggests (what is at once an evidence that the loss of fugitives is not a main ground for secession, and an argument against its practicability), that an everlasting border war must inevitably follow. Whether forts and sentinels be established or not, negroes would run off: they would be followed; and if across the line, very often the pursuers would be tempted to follow, and attempt their arrest and forcible return. This would be war, and could have no end as long as there was a slave within a hundred miles of the border. A sundering of the Union insures endless conflict, and the destruction of slavery along the boundary. Then the parts of States, from which it is thus driven away, will make a move for its entire abolition from the State, as Western Virginia has done, and as Missouri is doing. Thus there is no help for " the peculiar institutions of the South " in the empirical prescription of South Carolina.

But we have been told, time after time, " We'll secure the institution by treaty." What childishness ! The United States are to guarantee by treaty stipulations with the new Government the very institution whose protection was guaranteed in her Constitution—that very Constitution from whose protection secession tore herself away by the dismemberment of the nation ! This is one of the most preposterously absurd ideas that can be conceived ; and yet it has been frequently urged in my hearing by intelligent Virginians.

Personal liberty laws, so called, have been passed by some State Legislatures in the North, which have done much mischief ; not so much by their actual contents as by misconception of them in the South ; for there is not one of them in direct contradiction to the laws of Congress ; yet they in several instances betray a strong bias and wish in the Legislatures to do something in contravention of the Constitution and laws of the Union. They have gone as far as they dare go in this direction, and have thus proved themselves traitors to the Union in a moral sense. He who wishes to violate the law, and is restrained only by its penalties, is morally a transgressor. Legislatures who have pushed their repugnance to slavery to the very extreme, bordering upon conflict with the United States authority, have stained their hands with the blood of this civil war, and must answer for it to history and to God.

So, also, individual interference to prevent the execution of the laws of the United States, incurs this fearful responsibility. Blood hangs in the skirts of the men who murdered Kennedy at Carlisle Court House, and Gorsuch at Christina, in Lancaster county, Pa. Not only the direct perpetrators of these foul deeds, but the counsellors, the abettors and aiders of this resistance to law, and all who assisted in manufacturing the morbid public sentiment which goaded on these poor, ignorant blacks to these bloody deeds, are *participes criminis*, and have their account to settle with Him who judgeth righteously.

Whilst, however, we censure and deplore these assaults upon the laws of the States in the form of actual murder, and these acts of *quasi* treason against the United States, we nevertheless can see no reason in them all to justify rebellion. Law is better, always, than its execution; because the execution is in the hands of imperfect men. Proof against crime cannot be always made out legally. Many a jury has brought in a verdict of not guilty, while at the same time every man of them was convinced that the criminal perpetrated the murder. Moral evidence and legal evidence are not always identical. On the difficulties of executing the fugitive law, the reader will surely be gratified with a glance at a few more sentences from Mr. Everett:

" There is usually some difficulty in reclaiming fugitives, of any description, who have escaped to another jurisdiction. In most of the cases of fugitives from justice which came under my cognizance as United States Minister in London, every conceivable difficulty was thrown in my way, and sometimes with success, by counsel for the parties whose extradition was demanded under the Webster-Ashburton treaty. The French ambassador told me that he had made thirteen unsuccessful attempts to procure the surrender of fugitives from justice, under the extradition treaty between the two Governments. The difficulty generally grew out of the difference of the jurisprudence of the two countries, in the definition of crimes, rules of evidence, and mode of procedure."

The United States Government has done everything in its power, and never refused or failed, by its own fault, to protect the Constitution and all that it protects. The faults of individuals and of States are not chargeable upon it; and therefore there is not the shadow of a reason for rebellion against it on their account.

CHAPTER XXVIII.

THE RESTORATION.

THE design of these chapters is one—the preservation of our National Union. It is not their
purpose to detail a history of the rebellion; or
then many things must come in which are pur-
posely omitted. We should be obliged, in that
case, to inquire into the various somersets of Mr.
Calhoun, and especially his sad disappointment
and failure of getting the nomination for the Presidency—in fact, his history for the last thirty years
of his life; "The Partisan Leader," its plans and
plots; "the Knights of the Golden Circle;" and
Mr. Toombs' herculean labors in organizing these
secret clubs all over the South. Such was not our
purpose from the first; and we have introduced
history only as necessary in prosecuting our design,

and sustaining the hope of success in exposing the erroneous steps of reasoning by which the country has been brought into peril and suffering. That restoration is practicable, we have never permitted ourselves to doubt. The argument against this possibility, derived from the fact of war and all the evil passions to which it gives rise, is not based upon correct principles. It ignores the distinction between a public and a private enemy. It assumes the inveteracy of hostile feeling as a personal characteristic—that virulent antipathies are necessarily chronic, and therefore there is no reason to hope that the bitterness of this hate will ever pass away. We do not think so, and we will give our reasons.

1. Individual quarrels, involving the most bitter personal wrath, are not always permanent. Often two enraged men do the utmost violence to each other in trials of strength, and yet become friends again. The celebrated General Daniel Morgan was a great and notable fighter with the fist; he was real game at what, in the civilized nation of England, is called "the milling art." At the same place—Battletown, Va., so called because it was the grand rallying station of the buffers—lived a man named Bill Davis, greatly distinguished for his pugilistic prowess. These bullies eyed one another with great jealousy, fear, and hate for a

long time. At length the question, who was the
better fellow, came to the arbitrament of the fist—
rough and tumble ; and, after a struggle which
might put Dares and Entellus to the blush, Morgan (who, by the way, was a Pennsylvanian by
birth) was proclaimed victor. Now the agony is
over, and the fierce and mad antagonists shake
hands, take a little whiskey, and are better friends
than before. Such is human nature ; and the
world is full of examples of the same kind. Men,
individually, often whip themselves into respect for
each other. Morgan complimented Davis in strong
terms, as the most powerful man he ever took hold
of ; and Davis thanked him for the compliment :
coming from the hero of Battletown, he felt it was
the next thing to a triumph. And especially, after
Morgan returned from the fields of Revolutionary
strife, all hung around with laurels, Bill Davis
thought it an honor to have been whipped, after a
desperate struggle, by the hero of Quebec, Saratoga,
and a hundred other battles.

2. Thus has it been on a larger scale. Nations
respect each other the more for the very courage and
heroism which have caused them great loss of blood
and treasure. England had a far higher respect for
her late colonies, after she had felt the prowess
that slumbered in a peasant's arm—after Bunker

13

Hill and Yorktown and all that lay between them. The war of 1812 removed from the British mind the false notion, which had grown up in thirty years of peace—that English blood had become corrupt and degenerate in American veins; and the treaty of Ghent soon restored commerce and all the friendly relations of former times, and even more. Undoubtedly a higher regard for each other pervaded the recently hostile nations. Mexico and the United States are to-day more friendly than before the war between them. Such is the kindly feeling, that, beyond a doubt, but for our domestic troubles, we should say to Napoleon III—"Hands off, Sire! this continent is not for Frenchmen." How respectfully England, France, and Russia treat each other! Where is the rankling hate which it is supposed war necessarily engenders and perpetuates? No, it is gold, not gunpowder—commerce, not cannon, that creates permanent hostility between nations.

So, we have no doubt, it will be in our case. Before the outburst, one son of chivalry could whip five Yankees. "They shall acknowledge our independence, or we'll take Washington, march on to Philadelphia, take New York, and plant our banner over Faneuil Hall." All this gasconade has expended its force. They know now, that refusal to fight a duel is not proof of cowardice ; and we know that slavery does not insure such degeneracy as to disable men for the labors and hardships of the tented and the battle field.

The philosophy of all this is easily understood. In all such conflicts, individual and national, there are called into action physical powers that lay hid and whose existence was before unknown : there are developed intellectual energies that often astonish us ; and even moral properties that command our respect, admiration, and love. When a wounded enemy in the anguish of his heart cries for relief, and his foe divides his last cracker and his last gill of water with him, how can hatred rankle any longer in his soul ! When a strategetic movement, planned with skill and executed with energy, places one general and his army in the power of the other, what is there in the whole operation to engender hate ? What is there not to excite admiration and draw forth the highest respect ? And when the successful general uses his success honorably—soothes the feelings of his prisoner by kind and generous treatment, how can it result in anything else than an increase of kindly regards and a return to the amenities of Christian friendship ? Now these properties, physical, intellectual, and moral, are in themselves good ; and we cannot avoid admiring them, even in an enemy—yea, even when exhibited in the case of the highwayman and the pirate, although at the same time we despise the cause in behalf of which they are exercised. Now, let the cause perish, the properties still abide : the man who, as a foe, displays such excellent traits of character, I should like to have as a friend. The very reasons why I fear and hate him as an enemy, generate a desire to have him as a friend.

It may be said on the contrary, that acts of cruelty most barbarous have been extensively perpetrated, and wanton insults given beyond the possibility of pardon, and therefore the hope of reconciliation is as the giving up of the ghost. True, lamentably true, numerous instances of this character have disgraced the armies—at least partisans on both sides, and their tendency is undoubtedly against returning friendship. But after all, these are the exceptions ; the general conduct of the conflict has displayed a hundred acts of honorable and respectful treatment, for one of debased barbarism. The hundred, being common, arrest not attention, while the one act of brutality arouses indignation and renders the record ineffaceable. We can't forget it ; while the ordinary, generous conduct passes soon away. Besides, in most cases of this aggravated nature, the perpetrators are condemned by the great mass of their own side, even where they are not otherwise punished. *Ex uno, disce omnes*—is the basis of many a fallacy in reasoning : we cannot learn the character of all from that of one, until we have assurance that all are like the one. Goods sold by sample often disappoint the purchaser.

Another reason in favor of restoration is found in family connections. It is a family feud—so intended by its projectors, more than a quarter of a century ago. "The Partisan Leader," a bantling novel, of which Judge Beverly Tucker of Virginia was the father, John C. Calhoun of South Carolina the godfather, and Duff Green the dry nurse,—this bantling proclaimed this war to be a guerilla conflict, and made the leaders children of the same parents. The two Trevors, brothers, meet in deadly strife, and both perish, if I don't forget the wicked story. This has been substantially realized. Father and son, brother and brother, cousin and cousin, uncle and nephew, father-in-law and son-in-law have often met ; and possibly fallen by mutual wounds. But, then, the same relationships, and all others, exist in countless numbers, who, on both sides of this direful, fratricidal conflict, still live, and with palpitating heart yearn for peace and the restoration of the Union. These ties of kindred blood, I know, are kept at bay by the terrors of demagogy, so that they dare not speak out. But the moment it becomes safe, they will speak out, and rush together, and, locked in each other's arms, will defy the spirit of disunion to separate them evermore. The voice of nature will drown the mad cry of ungodly ambition.

Besides, as stated some time since, there never was a majority in the South deliberately in favor of separation. For example, Virginia twice decided by overwhelming votes against it ; first, in carrying the Whig ticket and appointing Bell and Everett electors ; and secondly in electing two thirds of the Union members to the convention. In this election, for further example, take Rockbridge county, where the average vote shows a fraction less than one out of eleven for the disunion ticket ; and yet, by dragooning and dragging, the slavetraders—a despised class, who raised one hundred thousand dollars for the purpose of corrupting and perverting the convention, combining with the one third minority and the Richmond junta that has always governed Virginia, succeeded in constraining a disunion vote from this Union convention. Toward this success, however, the guns against Sumter were a necessary contingent. Look at the dates. On the 13th of April,

1861, the convention, always sitting with closed doors, had gotten "into a tight place," as one of its members wrote me. Another of its members, Hon. Roger A. Pryor, went to Charleston to urge on the rebellion there, and was intensely engaged in that iniquitous work, pressing the assault upon the fort. This was deemed indispensable, as a means of forcing the convention to take sides with South Carolina. At half past four A. M. of the 13th the first gun was fired ; at half past nine of the 15th Major Anderson hauled down his flag and surrendered the fort. On the 17th the secessionists were in the majority and voted Virginia out of the Union. Then came the popular vote on the secession ordinance, preceded by Senator Mason's letter, virtually ordering all the freemen of Virginia who could not and would not vote secession, to leave the State. Thus were majorities created—thus a people, claiming to be free, were forced against their oft-expressed wishes—wishes expressed at the polls when no terror hung over them—were dragged out of the Union —a lion dragged at an ass's tail.

Now, can it be conceived that disunionists thus created will feel no inclination, when the terror of expulsion from their State, or extreme maltreatment in it, shall have been removed, to return to their first love, and again gladly range themselves under the banner of their country? Assuredly, when the deceptions practised upon them pass away —when the passions gotten up by such meretricious arts cease to distract their bosoms, the people will see their interest and their happiness in taking their proper place in the counsels of their nation, under the government created by their fathers, and sustained and participated in equally by themselves.

Then again, the drawing influences of a common Christianity they will not be able to resist. Throw all these cords of Christian affection over the ties of natural relationship, and the mighty attractions of an inherited patriotism, in whose glorious achievements all have a common and a deep and abiding interest, and we can hardly conceive an amount of repelling forces to counteract their contracting power.

Another ground of hope for a restoration will be found in whatever adjustment of the slave question shall be reached. For that some settlement will take place there ought to be no reasonable doubt. One scheme of adjustment I beg leave to re-present from a speech of mine, delivered on the first of July, 1856, before the Societies of Rutger's College, New Jersey, and printed by them. The subject is, "OUR NATIONAL POSITION." Toward the close, having referred to our Constitution and the

glorious system of our government under the figure
of a temple, the speech proceeds :

"Yes, fellow citizens, this magnificent temple
enshrines the temporal hopes of bleeding, groaning
humanity. The Siberian exile and the Russian
serf, the Hungarian and the Polish peasant, the
Austrian and the German boor, have heard of
American freedom, and sigh for its enjoyment. The
light of her shekinah has penetrated the dark
dungeons of the inquisition, and thrilled the bosom
of many a Copernicus, a Sylvio Pelico, and a
Madiai.

"Now, my friends, North and South—friends
of freedom, all ! shall this glorious Temple of Liberty—this *chef-d'œuvre* of the Almighty Architect,
this central attraction of an enslaved world—shall
it be hurled down and torn to atoms ? and, like another Bastile, by the deluded and misguided friends
of liberty ? Shall the stars and stripes which bear
your commerce and your thunder in triumph over
the waves of all the oceans, and float in sublime
majesty over yon magnificent temple, be trampled
in the mire and torn into ribbons, and worn in de-
rision beside the stars and garters of a titled despotism, in all the enslaved nations ? What say you ?
No ! The Union, it must be preserved.

13*

" What ought to be her doings ?   What does God, who placed us in this position, expect of us ?

" I answer, besides the duties enumerated, to be *Atlantic* and *Pacific*, like our own mighty oceans— to bear upon our shoulders the political heavens, and to quiet down the emotions of a sin-agitated earth.   The balance of power over the civilized world will then be in our hands.   Even now the opinion of America is a notable element in the deliberations of parliaments and cabinet councils the world over ; then no great question will be decided among the nations without our advice and consent. Toward the great Republic will all eyes turn before any modification of international law will be determined on.   American diplomatists will be of the quorum, whenever a congress of nations shall sit on the destinies of humanity.   Should it ever be otherwise, and should combinations of kingdoms be formed to crush out pure Christianity, and the liberty which it guarantees, a note from some future Milton, and under the direction of some future Cromwell at the head of the Republic, will arrest the march of armies and the sailing of navies.

" But now, my friends, this responsible, glorious, and proud national position, present and prospective, depends absolutely upon the preservation of our National Union.   That gone, the depth of our misery, degradation, and dishonor will be measured by the height of our felicity, grandeur, and glory.

" For thirty years our national position relative to the African race has appeared to me the grand providential problem of the nineteenth century. God is working out its solution, and glorious will be the result ; and the time of the end is near. Through the follies, crimes, and cruelties of Spain, Holland, Portugal, France, England, and America, there have been thrown upon this continent three millions of the race whom God hath painted black and brought hither. Why did God bring them ? Had He no wise purpose ? Does He work by guess ? If this is blasphemy, why brought He the African to these shores ?

" God's actual doings are the exponent infallible of His designs. ' What hath God wrought ? ' He hath Christianized more than three millions of His sable sons. A higher and a holier Christianity pervades this mass than does any equal mass of humanity on this globe, except in Britain and America. He has civilized as well as Christianized, in two hundred and thirty-six years, a larger proportion of human beings than have been civilized and Christianized by the agencies of all churches in the world for the last thousand years. These are facts of history, veritable as she has recorded on any section of her sphere.

" What, then, does God mean to do with the Africo-American race, just equal in number to the Israelites when they crossed the Red Sea, and to the American Colonies when they crossed the Red Sea of the Revolution in '76 ? What will He do with them ? Make use of them to pull down the temple of Liberty, and extinguish the hopes of the world ? Who believes it ? If, then, God cannot be guilty of such folly, what will he do with them ? Here, again, His doing is the expositor of His design. He will take them back to the place of their fathers' sepulchres in sufficient numbers to use them for the civilization and Christianization of a mighty continent. Here is the grand problem ; here its solution. Amid the griping lust of avarice and the lazy love of ease, and the rage of fanatical ignorance and stupidity, and the malignant plottings and schemings of corrupt, president-making demagogues, God is pressing toward the accomplishment of His own blessed and glorious plan for the regeneration and salvation of a continent. He is now making the wrath of man to praise Him, and when these agitations shall have brought the American people to a realizing apprehension of the difference between a war of revolution or a foreign war, and a civil war, which arrays a mighty nation one half against the other, He will restrain the remainder, and the people—not the demagogues and fanatics—but the mighty CHRISTIAN PEOPLE, will stay the sword, and say with one glad voice which will reverberate from ocean to ocean—' Ye are brethren, marching on toward the conquest of the world for its glorious Master ; see that ye fall not out by the way.' Let the human master exercise all his legal rights, but whenever God shall put it into his heart to send his servant home to his fatherland, let us furnish the means.

"Now, my respected audience, there is a way for the accomplishment of this work without danger of collision. Let each of the States pass the same law, requesting Congress to propose an extension of their power so as to remove existing doubts. Let the proposed amendment to the Constitution run thus : Congress shall have power ' To appropriate the sum of five millions of dollars annually for the removal to Africa of such colored persons as are free or may become free and are willing to go.' This would be but a revival in substance of Mr. Monroe's plan, which had, however, primary reference to recaptured Africans. It would leave the question of slavery itself, where God and the Constitution leave it, at the bar of individual conscience ; and it would give the United States no power over it whatever, while it would open a door for the return of captive Africa to his own land. Of course this movement must begin and be largely carried forward in the Southern States, before it would be advisable for the Northern to touch it. Should the South and the North unite and two thirds agree, the emigration of the free blacks would progress as fast as the safety of the two races could allow ; and when free people of color did not offer in sufficient numbers, Government might compound with their owners for the purchase ot others.

"This simple plan would accomplish three grand objects, each of which might be glory enough for one nation.

"It would restore to freedom in fact half a million of men, who are already nominally free, yet for ever tantalized and chafed to madness with the perpetual remembrance of their really degraded social and political position.

"It would civilize, and Christianize, and bring into life and actual being untold millions of their own race, for long ages lost to humanity in the deep and dark solitudes occasioned by the slave trade, and carry representative democracy and the English language in triumph over a vast continent.

"And it would save the Union. By transmuting all the bad passions which cluster around the slavery agitation, into a heaven-born charity, which aims to accomplish so stupendous and benevolent a work, it would create an emulation between the extremes of our American empire, whose thrilling energies in the cause of humanity and of God must reinstate, in its own masterly power, the great and glorious characteristic—we are many, we are ONE."

Let us merely mention, without expansion, the argument geographical. The Creator seems to have constructed the country for mutual dependence, and made it impossible for the North or the South, the East or the West, to be each independent of any or of all the rest. Interdependence will necessitate reunion, except on the Pacific. Here, iron rails are indispensable ; and the stronger bonds of brotherhood, Christianity and national patriotism.

CHAPTER XXIX.

THE BASIS OF RESTORATION.

RECONSTRUCTION, an expression often used in
the Senate chamber, and of which Senator Hunter
was peculiarly fond, presupposes entire dissolution,
and is therefore odious in our view. It implies the
pulling of the house down, because of such defects
as render its tenure dangerous, and the hope of
fitting it up by repairs, and thus rendering it ten-
antable, to have been abandoned. It is not, to be
sure, exactly like the leprous house of the Hebrew
law, when given over by the priest, to be utterly
rejected, in all its materials, as useless and forever
lost ; but the materials may still be partially
worked up in a new edifice. Some of them are to
be cast off entirely ; others, however, may, by the
new architects, be so reformed and dressed as to
occupy a place suitable to their inferior nature, in

some obscure parts of the grand, modernized structure.

Against all this, our feelings, we confess, revolt, and our judgment very decidedly objects. In the first place, we deny the assumption that the materials are decayed, unsightly, and unsuitable, to any such extent as to endanger the occupants of the building, or to deform its proportions, symmetry, or beauty. We have never believed it perfect in either of these respects. Doubtless some improvements are possible; but it makes abundant provision for these, without utter demolition. The principal defect apparent to our vision meets us at the very vestibule. The portico lacks one gem to perfect its lustre. *There* is Union and Justice, Common Defence and General Welfare, Blessing and Liberty; but we cast our eyes about in vain for that which alone can give stability and beauty to the whole — the Koh-i-noor, whose radiant glories crown the grandeur of the beautiful temple, the Shekinah, is absent. The grand bond of our National Union does not distinctly acknowledge the being of a God. For more than forty years, a 4th of July has seldom passed, on which I have not preached and warned my countrymen of this defect, and told them, if it be not supplied, God would pull down their temple and bury a nation in its ruins. This warning has been sounded forth from thousands of pulpits in the land, and would have been much more extensively trumpeted, but for the paralyzing influence of the fallacy—which we have already exposed—couched in the demagogue's double entendre, "Religion has nothing to do with politics." This defect has been supplied in the Constitution as reconstructed by the rebels. For this we give them honor due.

But, while we admit imperfection, and go in for amendments, we deny the necessity of reconstruction, and we do not believe it would be wise to proceed with amendments until after the restoration. Let that subject lie in abeyance until all the States return to their place in the Government and in subjection to the Constitution. There are other reasons why it should be so; and especially why there should be no dissolution, and, of course, no reconstruction. Among these we may set forth our defect in architectural skill. We have made little, no progress, in the seventy-three years that have passed since the building was completed. In naval architecture we have indeed shot ahead of our fathers and of the world; in civil and ecclesiastical construction and execution also we have far outstripped that age; and, indeed, in everything belonging to material advancement, the age has

been progressive, and the fathers have been left in
the rear threescore years and ten. The truth is,
the national mind has been so wholly absorbed in
the vast business of physical development and material advancement—we have been so fully alive to
the philosophy of material experiment, that the
higher studies of man—his nature, his intellectual
development, his laws of government, his moral
powers—have been relatively overlooked. The consequence is, the race of statesmen has died out,
and no new race has arisen to take their places.
We have no statesmen. Whither now will you
look for a Washington, an Adams, a Jefferson, a
Jay, a Hamilton, a Madison, a Franklin, a Pinckney, a Randolph? Manifestly, among the fossil
remains of an age gone by. We have no statesmen. . Politicians we have in scores; and demagogues, alas! in thousands; but statesmen, oh!
my country! where are they?

On the score of ability—abstract, intellectual
ability to build up a new system of government—
we therefore object to the attempt in this generation. But, if the capacity did exist, still more
seriously do we object on the ground of moral
qualities — of political integrity. Politics is a
grand rascal, and cannot be intrusted with reconstruction. The pure, unsullied patriotism of the

fathers, no man' expects to find, and, therefore, no man looks for it. All that is expected now is cunning, chicanery, tact in managing the wires, and skill in the tricks of party—the intrigues of faction.

What, then, is to be done ? Nothing—nothing at all ; but abide as you are—and you who have departed, return to your own natural position, where your fathers placed you. Exceedingly have I been grieved at a phraseology often used by speakers and writers, inadvertently, no doubt, in most cases. Men talk of conquering the South. My friends, this is all wrong. You cannot conquer the South—ten millions of people, or four millions of white freemen, cannot be conquered and kept down as a conquered people. This phraseology has done immense mischief already, and will produce much more. We of the United States do not desire to conquer the South. All we wish is, that the South return to their proper place—take their seats in the Senate, in the House, in the executive chair occasionally, in the departments, in the navy, in the army, in the customhouse, in the postoffice, in the diplomacy—in every place where the Constitution may and shall place them. Fight the armed rebellion we must ; break up hosts in hostile array against the flag we must ; but the suppression of an insurrection is not conquering a country. Let us not irritate our brethren by boasting and bragging about conquering them : we wish only to aid the Southern people, by suppressing the revolt, to return and place themselves under the ægis of the Constitution ; there to exercise all the rights and to enjoy all the privileges purchased by the blood and treasure of their fathers and guaranteed by this semi-inspired instrument. Here they have prospered, as we have seen from their own showing, beyond all examples in the world's history ; and here still more abundantly will they prosper after restoration. Experience teaches fools, and they are guilty of triple folly who cannot or will not learn even in the school of experience. We have all acquired much knowledge, within two years, that ought, if we be not unreasonably perverse, to lead us back to peace and harmony and love.

Plainly, then, the reader sees the basis of restoration in "the Constitution as it is and the Union as it was." In our humble opinion, there is no other rock on which the glorious temple of liberty can stand. Should the lightnings of heaven rive it, the building totters and falls ; and the hopes of freedom to man pass away as a tale that is told. Humanity, struggling forth from beneath the mighty ruin of representative democracy, will raise her bruised head and stretch forth her feeble hands imploringly, to despotism, seated on his iron throne, and pray for intervention to rescue her from the terrible grasp of a self-governed people.

CHAPTER XXX.

HAPPY CONSEQUENCES OF A RESTORED UNION.

FAMILY CONNECTIONS ALL OVER—BLESSED RETURN—NATIONAL
PROSPERITY—CHURCH REVIVED—MISSION AND BIBLE CAUSE
REGENERATED.

THE vast breadth of our territory—nearly equal
to the whole of Europe; the immense diversities of
its soil and climate, adapting it to almost all possible varieties of productions of the soil and the
mines; the countless variety of our population,
native and imported, insuring and enforcing endless diversities in tastes, capacities, and pursuits;
the perfect freedom of locomotion and cheapness of
land, attracting enterprise to all quarters—all these
have brought about such a perfect intermixture and
thorough dispersion of population and readjustment
of family ties by intermarriages where no class distinctions exist, as has never been exhibited on so
immense a scale since the dispersion at Babel.
There is scarcely a country on earth unrepresented
on this continent and in these United States.

Families must consist of few members and be of little enterprise, who have not branched forth into one, two, or half a dozen States. From the Atlantic shores they have flooded the West and the South. New England exists chiefly outside of herself. New York, after receiving an immense New England emigration, poured forth from her northern quarters multitudes over all the western regions, city and country; and from her southern quarters, her men and her capital into all the cities and regions from Baltimore to New Orleans and Texas. Her capital and men, along with those of New England, awoke up New Orleans and made it a commercial emporium. New Jersey left half her lands untilled and trooped away to the West. Pennsylvania, ignorant of her underground wealth—her iron and her coal, doomed shortly to dethrone King Cotton and to rule the world henceforth—flooded over the Potomac and filled up western Virginia, more than half of whose population hailed from the Quaker colony; then into Ohio and farther west. And still this interminable intermixture continues and increases. From all this it results that no great battle can be fought in this dire conflict, that does not find fathers and sons, brothers and brothers, cousins and cousins arrayed against each other. How intense the feelings of friends! how painful the anxieties of mothers and sisters and cousins, in dread apprehension of fratricidal slaughter ! What, then, must be their state of mind at the restoration ? With what palpitations of heart the mother and the sister will inquire of the returned soldier, son and brother, to be sure that his victories were not written out in the blood of a rebel son or brother ! When the glad sound of peace shall stay the uplifted sabre, just ready to fall and cleave a brother's skull ; or arrest the hand just at the moment when it is pulling the cord that must send the booming shell against the breast of a brother, a cousin, a father ; or stop the finger's motion, just as the sight is drawn for the face of a dear friend ; and when, in a few minutes more, the fact is revealed that the deadly movement must have struck down so dearly beloved a brother, father, friend—oh ! who can conceive the emotions of tenderness such a discovery must generate ? Who can describe with what transports of gratitude to God for such interposition, these enemies will throw down all hostile arms and rush into each other's warm embrace ? And then, friendly visits and reunion of long divided families ; and tearful reminiscences of mournful tragedies ; and confessions of regret and sorrow for the false logic which generated bad feelings ; and then, falling on their knees and pouring

14

out the most heartfelt thanks to God, that He has, through all these scenes of blood and carnage, carried so many of our dear ones safely, and brought us together before one family hearth and one common mercyseat. Oh yes, this dark night of sorrow and anguish will be followed by a bright morn and a joyful day.

To the nation many blessed consequences must follow in the train of peaceful restoration. It will have gone through the last trial needed to demonstrate the wisdom, power, and strength of the system contained in our Constitution. No government has ever been subjected to such a trial. No such conspiracy—for length of time in its preparation; for depth of cunning guided by such power of intellect; for extent of numbers engaged; for fiscal and physical resources; for diplomatic ingenuity and finesse; for clear insight into the pathological susceptibility (if I may use the expression) of the people to be stirred up and infuriated; above all, for overreaching sophistry— no such conspiracy has ever existed against any government on earth. If we can overcome this, and restore the Union as it was, and the Constitution as it is, that Union will be safe for a hundred years; and the principles of that Constitution will be secure forever; and all the nations of the

world may yet form one grand Republic under the
Stars and Stripes. We can see no serious obstacle
in the way of our unique principle of local governments to attend to local affairs, and a general
government based on the representative principle,
being applied for the world. The powers of Europe have for more than forty years been approaching, though slowly, toward this point. At the
close of the Napoleonic wars, the principal nations
held a congress of states and assumed the settlement of many great questions. Eloquently was it
said on that occasion, " Scarce has the soldier time
to unbind his helmet, and to wipe away the sweat
from his brow, ere the voice of mercy succeeds to
the clarion of battle and calls the nations from
enmity to love."

And does not the present disposition to inter-
vene in American affairs, bear the aspect of an
arbitration—a grand committee—a body of representatives for the adjustment of difficulties. Let a
star for old England, one for France, Russia,
Prussia, &c., be planted on the blue, and a congress of the whole earth may settle all controversies
by the arbitrament of reason and the ballot box.

Highly conducive to permanency and peace
will be found the amazing displays of energy and
power presented by this civil strife to the aston-

ished gaze of mankind. Such armies were never poured forth upon the ensanguined plain. Such desperate courage, such indomitable resolution, such strategetic skill, such profusion of men and money, such scientific energy in the construction of guns and ships, and all the appliances for destruction of life and property, the nations have never witnessed and history does not record. Now, when these stupendous powers shall have ceased their fratricidal direction; when they shall have coalesced under the old Flag, and a few years' rest shall have been taken to wear off acerbities and to heal all wounds; when we shall have become again, in heart and soul, One People, will it not be said of us, "God brought him forth out of Egypt; he hath as it were the strength of a unicorn; he shall eat up the nations his enemies, and shall break their bones, and pierce them through with his arrows. He couched, he lay down as a lion, and as a great lion: who shall stir him up?" Add to this our national growth. At the beginning of the twentieth century of our era, we shall count more than one hundred millions, and should our general advancement continue—should our resources run parallel with our population— and I can see no reason to doubt it, who shall stir up the old lion and the young? What nation

will assault the stars and stripes ? In what part
of the wide world will it not be adequate protection and secure respect to exclaim, I AM AN AMER-
ICAN ?

The cause of evangelical religion and the
churches of God in this land and in all lands, must
receive an immense impulse in connection with
this blessed restoration. I have before said, that
good men and true devoted servants of the Most
High—zealous, humble, pious men in great numbers, are spread all over the South. They fill the
legislative halls, the bench, the bar, the pulpit,
the church, the prayer meeting—yea, the army.
As holy and as true and zealous men as can be
found in the North, in Europe, or the world, are
engaged in this rebellion. I have labored to show
how they have been led into it—by violence done
to their reason, to their property, to their persons.
Bad men, too, and in great numbers, are spread with
equal diffuseness all over the South—men as false
and foul and fanatical as you can find in the
North—and this is saying a great deal. But the
counsels of Ahitophel will not always prevail :
the prayer has gone up from ten, fifteen, twenty
millions of hearts, and millions of millions of times
—hearts too that have power with God—"O Lord,
I pray thee, turn the counsel of Ahitophel into

foolishness." And it hath been heard, and it will be heard ; and his end, or rather the end of his disciples may be—"and hanged himself." Such a fate, probably, awaits such counsellors, North and South. But the people—the great body of the people, North and South, are not so, nor will they so end their career. They are true, sincere, and honest, and will lend all their energies to build again the walls of Zion which the Ahitophels have thrown down, and will restore the desolations of this generation.

With me it has long been a fond idea, that the Christian churches in this western land are destined of God to bear the banner of truth and righteousness over all the earth. Our civil institutions are based on the leading principle of the gospel plan of redemption—the principle of *representation.* It is worked into the warp and woof of our whole web of state and national policy. Having assumed as our fundamental principle that his Creator has vested in man the right and power of governing himself, we only need the idea of representation to render the exercise of the power practicable. Accordingly it is seen everywhere in actual operation ; and thus our religion becomes our politics—in the good sense—our statesmanship ; and our statesmanship becomes our religion. This

identity of principle and of its practical application
in government, both in church and state, qualify
this American people, above all on earth, to bear
the Christian religion and the freedom its doctrines
engender to all the families of the pagan nations.
The influence of this religion, in meliorating the
condition of society, in cultivating a peace policy,
in proclaiming good will to man everywhere, has
pervaded the entire mass of our population ; so
that the war spirit seems like a foreign element—a
deadly virus injected by the evil one into the life
circulation of our great body politic—a dangerous
disease gendered in the malaria of the Niger,
Senegal, and Senegambia. This the vigor of the
system will soon work out of the circulation and
throw off, when the entire renovated life will recu-
perate and perform its functions with increased
energy.

Our inexhaustible physical and, of course, fiscal resources constitute also an important element in the calculation of these forces. The
agricultural capacity of our lands is illimitable.
There is no possibility of exhausting our soil, under
our improving system of culture. On the contrary, there is a constant increase. Lands scuffled
over with the shallow-running old wooden plough,
the shovel scraper and the hoe, for a hundred

years, we are just beginning to discover, can be made to double or triple their product by kind and generous treatment. And when this triplicate ratio shall be reached, we shall discover that the process of improvement is but begun. It is no extravagance to suppose that our country will become thus adequate to a population of three hundred millions. In view of such resources, we cannot doubt the ability of this Christian nation to carry on the foreign wars—foreign to our American Christendom, but not to the dominions of our Prince—and to make the glad tidings of peace and salvation known to all the world. A tithe of the men and the money which we are now immolating at the altars of Mars, in consequence of the ungodly ambition of a few dozens of demagogues, would suffice, under the blessing of the Most High, to send a missionary, with the Bible in his hand, to every five thousand heathens in the world. What an argument the friends of missions and of Bible distribution will derive from this war! What member of the church, or of the civil community, will dare hereafter to excuse himself from a liberal contribution to the cause, on the ground of penury? Who will dare to deny the ability of the American people to conquer the world for Immanuel our Prince?

But let us not forget that missionaries and Bibles are not all that are necessary to insure this conquest. Oh, no. "Not by might, nor by power; but by my Spirit, saith the Lord." And here comes the solemn question: But will God give his Spirit, and thus insure the victory of truth and right? Can a nation of Christians, who have expended so largely their blood and treasure and energy in self-destruction, expect the Divine blessing in large measure? Will God, in very deed, dwell with men upon the earth? Will He, in very deed, make a suicidal nation the glorious instrument, in his own hand, of carrying out the purposes of his mercy to a lost world? Will he pour upon the American churches the spiritual gifts necessary to accomplish these stupendous results?

What God will do, of course, we can only learn from his word and from past movements of his holy providence. From these sources judging, we should expect great things. His chastising rod can fall upon his own children only in this world: when they leave it, they enter upon a state where there is no sorrow and sighing, because no sinning. The recent bitter experiences of the church, we hope, have produced some of the peaceable fruits of righteousness, for many of his people have been

14*

exercised thereby. Some humiliation and much prayer have gone up, North and South ; mingled, I fear, with many feelings, indeed, calculated to neutralize their effects. Still, there has been much sincere humiliation and heart-felt sorrow for our national sins—more supplication and inter-cession than at any period of our history. Now it is a settled principle in the Divine government, to chastise the individual and the nation no more than is sufficient to bring about a proper state of feeling ; a nation on its knees is likely to receive forgiveness ; but the measure of true penitential feeling, and of mere legal repentance, so to speak, necessary to justify the Divine government in a return to favorable dealing with it, is in His own hands. But His anger will not burn always : we look for the light of His countenance. We feel a high confidence that " He will turn the heart of the fathers to the children, and the heart of the children to their fathers ; " and ere long, not " smite the earth with a curse," but " pour out a blessing that there shall not be room enough to receive it." Contemporaneous with the restoration, we look for an effusion of the Spirit, such as the churches in this land have never witnessed. " I will pour upon the house of David and upon the inhabitants of Jerusalem the spirit of grace and of supplication : and they shall look upon me whom they have pierced [in the persons of my beloved children], and they shall mourn for Him as one mourneth for his only son ; and shall be in bitterness for Him, as one that is in bitterness for his firstborn. In that day shall there be a great mourning in Jerusalem, as the mourning of Hadad Rimmon, in the valley of Megiddon." Oh yes ! "All the families that remain, every family apart, and their wives apart." If such a day shall, through the united, earnest, and importunate prayers of his people, come upon the churches, then will Zion arise and shine, and the glory of the Lord shall be seen upon her : then shall this mighty people, with one heart and one soul, address themselves to the glorious work of evangelization, and distance all the nations in bearing the banner of the cross in triumph over all the legions of error and death.

From this point it is easy to see that countless blessings must follow to all the world from this restoration. Under the resistless influence of a heaven-born charity, let the boundless resources of this united and happy people be called forth, and directed to the amelioration of human condition, and what may not be the glorious results ? We have already stationed our sentinels on some of the most prominent points on the whole line of demarcation between the lands of darkness and the shadow of death and the regions of light and Christian civilization. The watch fires glimmer amid the solitudes and spiritual desolations of pagan superstition and Mohammedan delusion, and already the darkness perceptibly recedes, and the light expands its radiant circle. Oh, how shall it be, when not a few hundreds of devoted men and women are seen feeling their way toward a few chosen spots ; but tens of thousands shall rush forth, with lamps trimmed and oil in their vessels, to enlighten the earth ! How will not the light flash forth when, like Gideon's three hundred, these tens of thousands shall break their pitchers and hold their lamps aloft, crying, " The sword of the Lord and of Jesus ! " Oh, how will not the darkness flee away, and the Sun of Righteousness illumine the broad sky and awake the sleepers of earth to glory and immortality !

Then, the reflex influence of this spiritual illumination upon the civil institutions of the nations must be immense ; in reforming and elevating the masses ; in bringing down the loftiness of despotic rule ; in breaking off the heavy yoke of governments whose principle is the iron bondage of that fear which hath torment, and substituting in its

place the easy yoke of moral rule, under laws
founded in love that lightens all labor; in vindi-
cating to man the right of self-control, vested in
him by the God who made him; and in leading
him to the enjoyment of a well-regulated liberty,
founded on the Truth, and secured and promoted
by the governing principle of Representative Democracy.

APPENDIX.

———◦●◦———

Mr. JEFFERSON DAVIS, quite recently, demonstrated the separate independent sovereignties of the States, by the fact that the treaty of Paris, 1783, by which England acknowledged the independence of the United States, recites the States by name. Surely this gossamer sophism can entangle the intellectual limbs of no sane man. The fact is so. See Marten's *Recueil de Traites*, v. iii, 553. The heading is, "In the name of the Most Holy and United Trinity." The preamble recites the friendly disposition of the parties—"the Most Serene and Most Potent Prince, George the Third" and "the United States of America." It sets forth the object—"to establish such a beneficial and satisfactory intercourse between the two countries, upon the ground of reciprocal advantages and mutual convenience, as may promote and secure to both perpetual peace and harmony." "*Both* parties"—not fourteen parties, as Mr. Davis reads it, but the two, viz., the King of England and the United States; the very terms used in the treaty of Ghent in 1814.

"Art. I. His Britannick Majesty acknowledges the said United States, viz., New Hampshire, Massachusetts Bay, Rhode Island and Providence Plantations, Connecticut, New York, New Jersey, Pennsylvania, Delaware, Maryland, Virginia, North Carolina, South Carolina, and Georgia, to be free, sov-

creign, and independent States ; that he treats with them as
such, and for himself, his heirs and successors, relinquishes all
claim to the government, propriety and territorial rights of
the same and every part thereof." Mr. Davis's blunder—in-
tentional undoubtedly—consists in assuming that the States
are taken here *severally* and not jointly, as a *unit*. This is
not true, for the preamble and the very words of this article
calls them " the UNITED STATES," and *a party* to the treaty—
not *thirteen* parties. Obviously the naming of them severally
was necessary to exclude the other and contiguous colonies of
Great Britain—New Brunswick, Nova Scotia, and the two
Canadas; but all through they are considered as a unit—as
one people. This is demonstrably evident from the fact, that
Article II " defines the boundaries of the said United States."
This defining marks out the boundary of not one single State,
but only those of the whole thirteen as a unit—as one national territory—one country.

Art. III guarantees the right to take fish of every kind
* * * " to the inhabitants of both countries "—only two countries, not fourteen, are known.

Art. VII says, " all prisoners on both sides shall be set
at liberty." It also binds England to " leaving in all fortifications the American artillery that may be therein; and shall
also order and cause all archives, records, deeds, and papers
belonging to any of the said States or their citizens, * * * to
be forthwith restored, and delivered to the proper States and
persons to whom they belong." " Both sides"—two parties
only: and " the American artillery "—not the South Carolina,
the Pennsylvania, &c., artillery.

Art. X. " The solemn ratification of the present treaty
* * * shall be exchanged between the contracting parties in
the space of six months." Exactly so, in the treaty of Ghent,

the same phraseology occurs—His Britannic Majesty and the
United States of America: "Immediately after the ratification
of the present treaty by the two parties"—"all prisoners of
war taken on the one side or the other." And Art. VIII
speaks of the two parties: so X and XI speak of two sides
and the two parties.

The assumption of Mr. Davis that the States are severally
—each is acknowledged as a sovereign and independent power—is utterly groundless. England never treated any one of
them as a sovereign power; and General C. C. Pinckney, of
South Carolina, correctly flouts the idea "as a species of political heresy which can never benefit us, but may bring on us
the most serious distresses." See *ante*, p. 58.

INDEX.

THE END.